SUSTAINABLE DEVELOPMENT LAW

SUSTAINABLE DEVELOPMENT LAW

THE LAW FOR THE FUTURE

KARTIKEY HARI GUPTA

PARTRIDGE

To order additional copies of this book, contact
Partridge India
000 800 10062 62
orders.india@partridgepublishing.com

www.partridgepublishing.com/india

CONTENTS

Chapter I   Introduction 15

Chapter II   Principles of Sustainable Development 28

Chapter III International Law on Sustainable Development......................51

Chapter IV   Sustainable Development in Indian Legal Framework............79

Chapter V   Judicial Response... 112

Chapter VI   Sustainable Development Case Study of the Hydropower
             Projects in the State of Uttarakhand....................................... 168

	List of Tables and Figures	
No.	**Particulars**	**Pages**
Chapter I	Table 1: Challenges for a sustainable environment	17
	Table 2: Sources of energy identified by the CAG	22
	Table 3: Consumption of energy identified by the CAG	22
	Table 4: Micro hydro projects commissioned in the state	24
	Table 5: Micro hydro projects under construction in the state	25
	Table 6: Decentralised generation and distribution to the shrines	27
Chapter II	Table 1: Sustainable development principles under article 39 of the Constitution of India	42
	Table 2: ISDL principles	48
Chapter III	Table 1: 26 principles of the Stockholm Declaration, 1972	55
	Table 2: 27 principles of the Rio Declaration	60
	Table 3: Sections of Agenda 21	65
	Table 4: 'Seven Principles' of the International Law Association	73
Chapter IV	Table 1: Legislations in British India influencing the environmental, social, and economic development of natives	85
	Table 2: Facets of sustainable development principles enshrined in the Constitution of India	96
	Table 3: Sustainability factor identification and implementation route in the Twelfth Five-Year Plan (2012–2017)	108
	Table 4: Important Indian legislations in the area of sustainable development	110

Chapter VI	Figure 1: Sustainability and hydropower projects	169
	Figure 2: Balancing ecological protection with development of hydropower projects in the state	170
	Figure 3: Alienation of hydropower	171
	Figure 4: Impact of hydropower projects on ecosystem of the state	173
	Figure 5: Local area development due to hydropower projects	174
	Figure 6: The influence of hydropower projects on local ecology	176
	Figure 7: Development of state due to hydropower projects	178
	Figure 8: Large dams v. run-of-the-river projects (RoRs)/micro hydro projects (MHPs)	180
	Figure 9: Rehabilitation by the hydropower companies	182
	Figure 10: Postconstruction, HPPs undertake restoration of the loss of ecosystem	184
	Figure 11: Environmental clearance of hydropower projects	185
	Figure 12: Opinion regarding Indian courts' response to hydropower projects	186
	Figure 13: Opinion on court monitoring of construction activities of hydropower projects	189
	Figure 14: Government v. private hydropower projects	190

NO.	List of Cases	Page no.
1.	*Bandhua Mukti Morcha v. Union of India and Others,* AIR 1984 SC 802	113
2.	*Francis Coralie Mullin v. Union Territory of Delhi,* 1981 (1) SCC 608	114
3.	*Rural Litigation and Entitlement Kendra and Others v. State of Uttar Pradesh and Others,* AIR 1987 SC 359	114
4.	*Subhash Kumar v. State of Bihar and Others,* 1991 (1) SCC 598	115
5.	*Vellore Citizens Welfare Forum v. Union of India and Others,* 1996 (5) SCC 647	116
6.	*Indian Council for Enviro-Legal Action v. Union of India,* 1996 INDLAW SC 1073	119
7.	*Addl. Distt. Magistrate Jabalpur v. Shivakant Shukla,* AIR 1976 SC 1207	122
8.	Jolly George Varghese's case, AIR 1980 SC 470	122
9.	Gramophone Company's case, AIR 1984 SC 667	122
10.	*Chameli Singh v. State of UP,* 1996 (2) SCC 549	123
11.	*CESC Ltd. v. Subhash Chandra Bose,* 1992 (1) SCC 441	123
12.	*MC Mehta v. Union of India,* AIR 1997 SC 734	124
13.	*Indian Council for Enviro-Legal Action v. Union of India,* 1996 (5) SCC 281	124
14.	*AP Pollution Control Board II v. Prof. M. V. Nayudu (Retd.) and Others,* 2001 (2) SCC 62	125
15.	*T. N. Godavarman Thirumalpad v. Union of India and Others,* AIR 2003 SC 724	125
16.	*N. D. Jayal and Another v. Union of India and Others,* AIR 2004 SC 867	129
17.	*State of Himachal Pradesh v. Ganesh Wood Products,* 1995 (6) SCC 363	130
18.	*M. C. Mehta v. Kamal Nath,* 1997 (1) SCC 383	130
19.	*Essar Oil Limited v. Halar Utkarsh Samiti and Others,* 2004 (2) SCC 392	130

20.	*Intellectuals Forum, Tirupathi v. State of Andhra Pradesh and Others*, AIR 2006 (SC) 1350	133
21.	*Glanrock Estate (Pvt.) Ltd. v. State of Tamil Nadu*, 2010 INDLAW SC 746	134
22.	*T. N. Godavarman v. Union of India*, Writ Petition No. 202 of 1995	135
23.	*Ramgopal Estates Private Limited v. State of Tamil Nadu and Others*, 2007 INDLAW MAD 964	136
24.	*Intellectual Forum v. State of AP*, 2006 (3) SCC 549	138
25.	*Godavarman v. Thirumal Pad, Tamil Nadu*, 2002 (10) SCC 606	138
26.	*N. D. Jayal v. Union of India*, 2004 (9) SCC 362	138
27.	*Vedanta Aluminium Limited v. Union of India and Others*, 2008 (2) SCC 222	142
28.	*Matri Sadan through Its Trustees and Others v. Himalaya Stone Crusher Private Limited and Others*, 2011 INDLAW UTT 662	143
29.	*State of Bihar v. Kedar Sao*, 2003 INDLAW SC 651	143
30.	*Sri M. C. Mehta v. Union of India*, 1997 (3) SCC 715	143
31.	*Milk Producers Association, Orissa and Others v. State of Orissa and Others*, 2006 (3) SCC 229	144
32.	*Research Foundation for Science Technology and Natural Resource Policy v. Union of India and Others*, 2007 (15) SCC 193	144
33.	*Reliance Natural Resources Limited v. Reliance Industries Limited*, 2010 INDLAW SC 347	145
34.	*State of Uttaranchal v. Balwant Singh Chaufal and Others*, AIR 2010 SC 2550	146
35.	*Karnataka Industrial Areas Development Board v. Sri C. Kenchappa and Others*, AIR 2006 SC 2038	146
36.	*Maharashtra Land Development Corporation and Others v. State of Maharashtra and Another*, 2010 INDLAW SC 954	147
37.	*Lafarge Uranium Mining Private Limited, T. N. Godavarman Thirumulpad v. Union of India and Others*, AIR 2011 SC 2781	147

38.	*Narmada Bachao Andolan v. Union of India and Others*, 2000 10 SCC 664	148
39.	*Centre for Public Interest Litigation and Others v. Union of India and Others*, 2012 INDLAW SC 29	149
40.	People's Union for Civil Liberties v. Union of India and *Others*, Supreme Court of India, Record of Proceedings, available at http://www.sci.nic.in/, last visited on 9 October 2012	150
41.	Re: Special Reference No. 1 of 2012, 2012 (10) SCC	150
42.	*Bharat Jhunjhunwala v. Managing Director, National Hydroelectric Power Corporation and Others*, Writ Petition (PIL) No. 211 of 2008, filed in the Hon'ble High Court of Uttarakhand at Nainital	151
43.	Indian Council for Enviro-Legal (ICELA) v. Union of *India and Others*, Writ Petition (PIL) No. 468 of 2008 in the High Court of Uttarakhand at Nainital	151
44.	Rural Litigation and Entitlement Kendra (RLEK) v. *State of Uttarakhand and Others*, Writ Petition (PIL) No. 532 of 2008 in the High Court of Uttarakhand at Nainital	152
45.	Rural Litigation and Entitlement Kendra v. Union of *India, Rural Litigation and Entitlement Kendra (RLEK) v. Union of India*, Writ Petition (PIL) No. 15 of 2009 in the Hon'ble High Court of Uttarakhand at Nainital	152
46.	National Thermal Power Corporation v. Union of *India and Others*, Writ Petition No. 2455 of 2011 in the High Court of Uttarakhand	156
47.	*NTPC Ltd. v. State of Uttarakhand*, Writ Petition No. 2607 of 2011 (M/S) filed on 13 December 2011 in the Hon'ble High Court of Uttarakhand	158
48.	*Jaiprakash Associates Limited v. State of Uttaranchal*, AIR 2007 (Utt) 41	159
49.	*Alaknanda Hydro Power Co. Ltd. v. Anuj Joshi and Others*, Civil Appeal No. 6736 of 2013 judgement dated 13 August 2013. at www.sci.nic.in	162

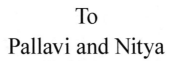

To
Pallavi and Nitya

PREFACE

Development is the most perennial facet of earth. It was taking place even when humans were not measuring it in the time frame. Since then, the development of human civilisations started being measured, and then perhaps we realised that our resources are not unlimited. And we began to be conscious about nature.

Only when equality- and equity-based distribution of resources is ensured, when social well-being is prioritised in the collective efforts of a society, and when ecological and environmental protection is made a preliminary requirement or a basic ingredient of all growth models, sustainable development is possible. Without ensuring a fine balance amongst social upliftment, economic growth, and environmental protection sustainability of development cannot be ensured. Contemporary jurisprudence has very recently recognised the role of social and economic factors in the overall developmental process. Environmental and ecological protection is often mentioned in sustainable development jurisprudence.

This study tries to answer the burning issue of today's times (i.e. right to development versus right to environment). In a state like Uttarakhand, where even basic medical and educational facilities are a distant dream, sustainable development is seen in some different context from rest of the world. The state of Uttarakhand, especially its remote areas and remote people, needs to be made part of mainstream globalisation and growth.

Harmonious coexistence is the core of the concept of sustainable development, encompassing both natural and man-made environments. Development must be sustained by future generations. We cannot grow haphazardly; we have to develop equitably. The concept of intergenerational equity and a transanthropocentric approach should be given prime importance while drawing up any developmentalactivity.

The principle of sustainable development provides a harmonious balance between environment, economy, and society with that of economic growth and social development. Each and every ecosystem in which humans interact for development has its carrying capacity. This principle mandates that while endeavouring for economic growth and social development, attention should be given to the carrying capacity of the ecosystem.

The principle of intergenerational equity is the first principle which implies a duty of the present generation towards future generations. The origins of the second principle—the public trust doctrine—are traceable to Roman law concepts of common property. Under Roman law, the air, the rivers, the sea, and the seashore are incapable of private ownership; they are dedicated to the use of the public. The third principle is known as the precautionary principle, which is more precisely elucidated in principle 15 of the Rio Declaration of 1992; it declares the following: 'Where there are threats of serious or irreversible environmental damage, lack of full scientific certainty should not be used as a reason for postponing measures to prevent environmental degradation.' The principle of extended producer responsibility is commonly known as the polluter pays principle. The underlying idea of the polluter pays principle is that those who damage the environment should bear the cost of such damage.

In the case of *Hinch Lal Tiwari v. Kamala Devi and Others*, the principle of equity- as well as equality-based distribution of resources has been dealt with. It was held in this case that 'it is important to notice that the material resources of the community like forests, tanks, ponds, hillock, mountain etc. are nature's bounty. They maintain delicate ecological balance. They need to be protected for a proper and healthy environment which enables people to enjoy a quality life which is the essence of the guaranteed right under Article 21 of the Constitution'. With the advent of the modern ideas of equality and infusion of sustainability jurisprudence in the law-making process, the Constitution of India (vide in its article 39) also provided the policy of sustainable development to be adopted by the state. The state is the legal owner and trustee of its people, and it must ensure that the process of distribution is guided by the doctrine of equality and greater public good. Sustainable development can happen only when it happens for all. Right to livelihood has been declared by the constitutional courts of India as part and parcel of the fundamental right to life guaranteed under article 21 of the Constitution of India. To ensure the fundamental right to livelihood is fundamental to state policy, and it must be ensured through the equitable distribution of resources.

When it comes to the principle of sustainable state and governance, a sustainable state with equally sustainable governance is the next stage of development, moving ahead from the liberal state. Most modern and contemporary states are not only concerned with the welfare of their people but also have taken up the task of ensuring the fair processes of justice and good governance. Seven *core principles* of international sustainable development law (ISDL) were identified by the New Delhi Declaration as the following:

- Principle 1: the duty of the states to ensure sustainable use of natural resources
- Principle 2: the principle of equity and eradication of poverty
- Principle 3: the principle of common but differentiated responsibilities
- Principle 4: the principle of the precautionary approach to human health, natural resources, and ecosystems
- Principle 5: the principle of participation and access to information and justice
- Principle 6: the principle of good governance
- Principle 7: the principle of integration and interrelationship (in particular, in relation to human rights and social, economic, and environmental objective)

The beginning of international framework for sustainable development can be traced to the UN Conference on the Human Environment held in Stockholm. The Stockholm Declaration was the pioneer in explicitly recognising the right to a healthy environment. It places importance on protecting both species and their habitat. The outcome of the conference was the statement on the Declaration on the Human Environment that contained 26 principles and 109 recommendations which are commonly referred to as the Stockholm Declaration. The development of international environmental law is attributed to the Stockholm Declaration.

Commonly known by its chair Gro Harlem Brundtland, the World Commission on Environment and Development (WCED) was convened by the United Nations in 1983, and its report named 'Our Common Future' was published in 1987. The Report of the Brundtland Commission came up as 'Our Common Future', and this report defined the concept of sustainable development as 'sustainable development is development that meets the needs of the present without compromising the ability of future generations to meet their own needs. It contains within it two key concepts: "the concept of needs, in particular the essential needs of the world's poor, to which overriding priority should be given"; and "the idea of limitations imposed by the state of technology and social organization on the environment's ability to meet present and future".'

World leaders met in Rio de Janeiro at the United Nations Conference on Environment and Development (UNCED) in June 1992 for a summit widely known as Earth Summit. Marking the twentieth anniversary of the Stockholm Conference, members of the Earth Summit adopted the Rio Declaration on Environment and Development. The Rio Declaration contained twenty-seven principles of sustainable development, including principle 7 on 'common but differentiated responsibilities'. The outcome of the conference (in particular, Agenda 21 and the Rio Principles) became instrumental in promoting the development and strengthening of institutional architecture for environmental protection and sustainable development at the national and international levels. In all, the Rio Declaration contained twenty-seven principles of sustainable development.

The year 1992 saw the convening of the Earth Summit to address urgent problems regarding environmental protection and socioeconomic development. It saw the signing of the Convention on Climate Change and the Convention on Biological Diversity, endorsed the Rio Declaration and the Forest Principles, and adopted Agenda 21, a 300-page plan for achieving sustainable development in the twenty-first century. As a result of this landmark summit, the Commission on Sustainable Development (CSD) was created to monitor and report on the implementation of the Earth Summit agreements. All the nation heads reiterated their conviction that the achievement of sustainable development requires the integration of its economic, environmental, and social components and also recommitted to working together in the spirit of global partnership to reinforce their joint efforts to meet equitably the needs of present and future generations.

The Millennium Summit in September 2000 was called under the aegis of United Nations, which resulted into the largest gathering of world leaders in history. This also led to the adoption of the UN Millennium Declaration, which committed to a new global partnership to reduce poverty and setting out a series of time-bound targets (eight goals) with a deadline of the year 2015. Through the Millennium Development Goals (MDGs), for the first time, the world provided for itself time-bound and quantified targets for addressing extreme poverty in its many dimensions, such as income poverty, hunger, disease, and lack of adequate shelter; and it committed itself to the promotion of gender equality, education, and environmental sustainability. MDGs were recognised as basic human rights as the rights of each person on the planet to health, education, shelter, and security.

A decade after the Earth Summit held in Rio de Janeiro, the Earth Summit also referred to as Rio+10 was held in September 2002 in Johannesburg, South Africa. The Johannesburg Declaration and the Plan of Implementation of the World Summit on Sustainable Development were the main outputs of the summit. It is a successor to the UN Conference on the Human Environment at Stockholm in 1972 and the Earth Summit in Rio de Janeiro in 1992. While being a move towards committing states to uphold sustainable development, it looked at multilateralism as the way ahead. The Johannesburg Plan of Implementation, which was agreed to at the World Summit on Sustainable Development in 2002, recognised and reaffirmed these principles. It said, 'We strongly reaffirm our commitment to the Rio Principles, the full implementation of Agenda 21 and the Program for the Further Implementation of Agenda 21.' The Johannesburg Plan of Implementation identified following workable areas of sustainable development: (a) poverty eradication, (b) changing unsustainable patterns of consumption and production, (c) protecting and managing the natural resource base of economic and social development, (d) sustainable development in a globalising world, (e) sustainable development of small island developing states, (f) sustainable development for Africa and others. It further identified the means of implementation for sustainable development and began with the 'the principle of common but differentiated responsibilities'. The Johannesburg Plan of Implementation, as agreed to at the World Summit on Sustainable Development in 2002 (WSSD 2002), made a tectonic shift in the plan of sustainable development. It moved the world sustainable development jurisprudence from mere environmental concern and issue towards social and economic development. Rio+10 resulted in the integration of the MDGs with sustainable development principles and practices.

The Rio Declaration was followed by the 'Report of the Expert Group Meeting on Identification of Principles of International Law for Sustainable Development'. This report, which was released in September 1995, identifies nineteen principles and concepts of international law for sustainable development based on the Rio Declaration, Agenda 21, international treaties, and other legal instruments. Following up on the recommendations of the report, the Committee on the Legal Aspects of Sustainable Development of the International Legal Association (ILA) released its New Delhi ILA Declaration on Principles of International Law Relating to Sustainable Development as a resolution of the 70th Conference of the International Law Association in New Delhi, India, on 2–6 April 2002. (The ILA has consultative status, as an international non-governmental organisation, with a number of the United Nations specialised agencies.) The declaration noted that sustainable development is now widely accepted as a global objective and that the concept has been amply recognised in various international and national legal instruments, including treaty law and jurisprudence at international and national levels. It outlines seven principles of international law on sustainable development.

In pursuance of the General Assembly resolution, the United Nations Conference on Sustainable Development (UNCSD) was organised in Brazil on 20–22 June 2012 to mark the twentieth anniversary of the 1992 UNCED in Rio de Janeiro and the tenth anniversary of the WSSD 2002 in Johannesburg; for these reasons, this conference is also known as Rio+20.

Sustainable development finds elaborate mention in ancient Indian jurisprudence. The whole idea of living was based on the harmonious coexistence with nature. In India, a high regard for traditions has ensured that the sustainable development values are incorporated into the social and legal norms of modern society.

Written by Kautilya, the prime minister of the Mauryan empire, the *Arthashastra* is an ancient Indian treatise on politics and governance. Although it is basically about governance and the rights and duties of the kings and princes, it also serves as a guide on how various sections of society should be taken care of. Principal provisions relating to the environment are in book 2. The king has been ordained to set up new forests. Wildlife was regarded as very important in the Mauryan empire. The concepts of reserve forests and separate pathways for wildlife were there. In chapter 26, various punishments have also been provided for the person who kills animals under state protection. Social, economic, and environmental concepts—all three components of modern-day sustainable development—find adequate mention in ancient Indian life.

The policy of Dhamma included the state's concern for the welfare of its people. The emperor claims, 'On the roads I have had banyan trees planted, which will give the shade to beasts and men. I have had mango groves planted and I have had wells dug and rest houses built every nine miles . . . And I have had many watering places made everywhere for the use of beasts and men. But this benefit is important, and indeed the world has enjoyed attention in many ways from former kings as well as from me. But I have done these things in order that my people might conform to Dhamma (Pillar Edict VII, translated by Romila Thapar).' The state had a responsibility to protect and promote the welfare of not only its people but also its wildlife.

The state's primary concern became the principles of sustainable development in the form of social welfare and economic well-being of subjects. The state instructed the general public to show special care and concern for forests, wildlife, and other natural habitats through edicts placed on various rocks.

Colonial rules mainly exploited the colonies and overlooked their welfare. No exception to the rule was the British rule in India. A prominent concern in all policy decisions was the exploitation of natural resources. Any concern for the environment or any care for the economic well-being could not be seen in the colonial policies. However, the silver lining was in the form of certain laws that incidentally benefitted the colonial population. Under the influence and pressure of local leaders, the British put into force various laws that helped in the social development of the people of India. The colonial mindset of the rulers are explicitly seen in the National Forest Policy of 1894, the first formal forest policy in India. This policy stipulated that 'forests which are the reservoirs of valuable timbers should be managed on commercial lines as a source of revenue to the States'.

The Constitution of India is the *Grundorm* of sustainable development. One of the most prominent features of the Indian constitution is that it talks about the composite development of the people. Social and economic development are expressly secured in the legal framework of India. Protection and improvement of the natural environment saw the express provision in the Constitution of India for the first time in the form of the fundamental duty of a citizen enshrined in article 51A of the constitution. The Indian courts have read and interpreted the environmental aspect as a natural corollary to various other provisions of the constitution.

Post-independence, India adopted the method of development through planning, and various plans at five-year intervals were formulated and implemented. These plans are the source of policy formation and the guiding principles for the legislation at the different stages of federal structure in India. Environment sustainability became evident from Fourth Plan onwards in India. The most relevant for us today for the sustainability paradigm are the ideas and projections of the Twelfth Five-Year Plan of the government of India. For the first time in India, the Twelfth Five-Year Plan has given the idea of estimating green national accounts, which would measure national production while allowing for negative effects on national resources. This would be the indicator of the real gross domestic product (GDP) of the country.

The Indian parliament too has shown immense concern towards sustainable development principles. Legislative enactments were always coloured with the principles of economic and social security. Keeping pace with international commitments, the Indian Parliament passed various laws effecting and regulating environmental issues. India also gained credit as the first country that made provisions for the protection and improvement of the environment in its constitution. By way of forty-second amendment to the constitution in year 1976, directive principles of state policy in chapter 5 of the constitution as Article 48-A was inserted, which enjoins the state to endeavour for the protection and improvement of the environment and the safeguarding of the forests and wildlife of the country. Another landmark provision with respect to the environment was also inserted by the same amendment as article 51-A (g) of the constitution as one of the fundamental duties of every citizen of India. It stipulates that it shall be the duty of every citizen of India 'to protect and improve the natural environment including forests, lakes, rivers and wild life and to have compassion for living creatures'.

Judicial Response

By relaxing the traditional rule of standing (*locus standi*), the Apex Court of India gave birth to a new era of public interest litigation. Majority of the judicial response to the omissions and commissions of the legislature as well as executive in the field of sustainable development jurisprudence has been corrected by way of public interest litigation by the Hon'ble Supreme Court of India. Various measures for social upliftment and the improvement of the well-being of the downtrodden sections of society have been taken by Indian courts through public interest litigation. It is through the public interest petitions that the courts have recognised the concept of 'representative standing' in a *lis*.

The PIL(Public Interest Litigation) is characterised by a collaborative problem-solving approach. Acting either at the instance of petitioners or on their own, the supreme court has invoked article 32 of the constitution to grant interim remedies, such as stay orders and injunctions, to restrain harmful activities in many cases. Reliance has also been placed on those in power to do complete justice under article 142 to issue detailed guidelines to executive agencies and private parties to ensure the implementation of various environmental statutes. In *Bandhua Mukti Morcha v. Union of India and Others*, J. Pathak, while concurring, held that 'public interest litigation in its present form constitutes a new chapter in our judicial system. It has acquired a significant degree of importance in the jurisprudence practised by our courts and has evoked a lively, if somewhat controversial, response in legal circles, in the media and among the general public'. In the matter of *Rural Litigation and Entitlement Kendra and Others v. State of Uttar Pradesh and Others*, the Hon'ble Supreme Court, while emphasising the importance of article 51 (g) of the Constitution of India, held 'preservation of the environment and keeping the ecological balance unaffected is a task which not only Governments but also every citizen must undertake. It is a social obligation and let us remind every Indian citizen that it is his fundamental duty as enshrined in Article 51 A (g) of the Constitution'.

While streamlining the remedy of public interest litigation for the protection of the environment, Justice K. N. Singh writing for himself and for Justice N. D. Ojha in the case of *Subhash Kumar v. State of Bihar and Others* held that the 'right to live is a fundamental right under Art 21 of the Constitution and it includes the right of enjoyment of pollution free water and air for full enjoyment of life. If anything endangers or impairs that quality of life in derogation of laws, a citizen has right to have recourse to Art, 32 of the Constitution for removing the pollution of water or air which may be detrimental to the quality of life. A petition under Art. 32 for the prevention of pollution is maintainable at the instance of affected persons or even by a group of social workers or journalists'. Jurisprudence on the matters of environmental protection and sustainable development was foremost discussed by Hon'ble Justice Kuldeep Singh while delivering judgement in the matter of *Vellore Citizens Welfare Forum v. Union of India and Others*. In the judgement giving way to international sustainable development principles to be followed in the Indian domestic legal arena, it held the following: 'The traditional concept that development and ecology are opposed to each other, is no longer acceptable. Sustainable Development is the answer.'

Since its formation of the state of Uttarakhand, its people have undertaken various development initiatives. Uttarakhand is a very rich state in terms of natural resources. Hydropower has been one of the key areas in which considerable development has been done by the state. The most successful hydropower project of the state is Tehri Hydro Power Project. Hydropower projects are similar in nature to high dams with large generation capacity and small run-of-the-river projects. The small run-of-the-river projects have been encouraged by the state due to their sustainability and community-friendly aspects.

With the setting up of various large and small river water dams in the state of Uttarakhand also came sustainability concerns. River Ganga is also considered very sacred by a large portion of India's majority Hindu population. After the creation of a separate state of Uttarakhand, majority of the old hydropower projects gained momentum. As part of its policy to be an energy-surplus state, the government of Uttarakhand also encouraged many small hydropower projects on the river Ganga or on its various tributaries. Government public sector undertakings (PSUs) like the National Thermal Power Corporation (NTPC) and UJVNL (Uttarakhand Jal Vidyut Nigam Ltd.), as well as private players like GVK Shrinagar Hydro Electric Project adopted a very aggressive approach towards the construction of hydropower projects and their commissioning. Parallel to the construction of hydropower dams, the mass movement of local people also started. A large fraction of people of the hill state protested against the haphazard construction activities in the area. A legal battle for sustainability for power projects in the state also reached the constitutional courts of the state. While lengthy legal battles were going on in the constitutional courts of the state between environmentalists and development activists, the union government decided to establish a special National Ganga River Basin Authority(NGRBA) for a sustainability review of all river water projects on the River Ganga. The government of India constituted the National Ganga River Basin Authority (NGRBA) on 20 February 2009 under section 3(3) of the Environment (Protection) Act of 1986 and has also given Ganga the status of a national river. NGRBA is a specialised body for the comprehensive management of the River Ganga Basin, and its mandate is to ensure development requirements in a sustainable manner to ensure ecological flows in the Ganga. The constitution of the NGRBA is very comprehensive and high powered too.

During our empirical study of court cases touching upon the issues of the construction of hydropower projects in the state of Uttarakhand, one peculiar aspect emerged. It was noted that the major litigation happened not against the government or its subsidiaries but amongst the government and its instrumentalities. During the interviews of officers of the public sector companies involved in the hydropower generation in the state of Uttarakhand, it was felt as if they were totally disconnected from the government machinery and seemed not to have any better coordination and cooperation with government agencies than other private sector companies involved in the area.

In Uttarakhand, excessive rainfall and inclement weather during the middle of June 2013 resulted in a monumental tragedy. A large number of people living alongside the river and in hilly regions of the state witnessed nature in its very cruel state, and a large number of people were left homeless and displaced. The approximate number of villages affected was 1,603, with 1,08,653 people directly affected and 4,726 houses fully damaged. Keeping in view of the situation, the Ministry of Water Resources (MoWR) established the Ganga Flood Control Commission to identify the causes for the severe damage in Uttarakhand due to flooding and erosion during 16–17 June 2013. This committee submitted a detailed report to the government with reasons for such a massive disaster caused by severe weather conditions and also suggested preventive measures. Flood moderation by the Tehri reservoir found special mention in the report of the committee as follows:

> One of the conclusions reached by the abovementioned committee is very crucial for this research and that is clearly in favour of the construction of large dams like Tehri Dam in the State of Uttarakhand.

The above said conclusion and consequent recommendation is quoted below:

> Conclusion No. 5: It is evident that the existence of large storage in Tehri Dam was helpful in absorbing a substantial amount of flow in Bhagirathi River. The flood situation in the reach downstream of Devprayag could have been further worse in absence of Tehri Dam. The highest observed discharge in river Ganga at Haridwar was about 5.25 cusec during the current episode. This could have been more than 6.5 lakh cusecs in the absence of Tehri Dam.
>
> Recommendation No 4: Construction of large storages, wherever feasible, on Alaknanda/Mandakini/Pindar headstream of the Ganga river system. These storages could be operated in a manner to provide opportunity for absorption of flood in unfavourable condition. Possibility of storage on tributaries may also be explored.

Many people support the idea of hydropower because it is the most sustainable form of energy production and its necessity for sustainable development. While voting hydropower as being the cleanest form of energy, any preference in favour of coal, gas, or nuclear power has been categorically denied by majority of voters. Contrary to the fact that usable coal and gas are already in short supply, hydropower is as perennial as river water itself and is regarded as a sustainable means for energy production.

The calamity in the state in the year 2013has brought to the forefront the connection between development and natural calamities. The increasing pressure on natural resources has often resulted in threats to the fragile ecosystems. When asked if hydropower projects were threatening the fragile ecosystems of the state, 61 per cent of the respondents replied in the affirmative. Meanwhile, 62 per cent stated that natural river systems were facing threats due to many hydropower projects. It goes on to show that the haphazard construction of substandard projects cannot be a solution for the energy needs of the state. Residents of the state are equally sensitive about the fragile ecosystem of the state and also have a high regard for its natural river systems. Apart from the demand of maintaining the minimum flow in the rivers, it is imperative on the part of hydropower companies to have a sustainable view of the utilisation of the state's natural resources. Mere profit motives cannot guide hydropower companies.

An ambiguity remains in understanding whether government companies provide better opportunities and ecology support than private companies. In Uttarakhand, hydropower projects have been established by both government as well as private sector companies, such as NTPC, GVK, NHPC, etc. When respondents of Uttarakhand were asked if government agencies construct hydropower projects in a more eco-friendly manner, 46 per cent replied positively. When asked if private companies are more responsible for pollution than government agencies while doing construction of hydropower projects, 62 per cent replied in the affirmative. In regard to better rehabilitation and compensation being provided vis-à-vis private and public companies, 30 per cent replied with a yes, 37 per cent with a no, and 33 per cent did not have an answer for the same. The rehabilitation and resettlement offered by companies due to dislocation as a result of hydropower projects needs to be based more on needs and should provide the same opportunities and resources in the communities as before. Rehabilitating communities without providing them economic and social avenues could pose a threat to their very existence.

Since no scientific study exists on the issue, it would be unjust to arrive at a conclusion that hydropower projects were the main cause of devastation in the state during 16–17 June 2013.

However, it cannot be ignored that haphazard activities and construction of any kind—be it the hydropower projects in the valley, heavy silting of construction material on riverbanks, unscientific blasting activity by construction companies, and also the heavy encroachments of human settlements on the riverbanks—are the primary reasons behind such disasters.

Finally, the conclusions of the present study are that 'what must be stalled is the violation of the existing laws and safeguards, what must be controlled is the unscientific blasting of hills, what must be stopped is haphazard dumping of the construction debris on the riverside, what must be checked is the collusive corruption of construction companies with the local as well as state administration, what must be condemned is the never ending greed and insatiable hunger of private construction companies for profits and ; not the development of hydro-power per se in the state, not the right to livelihood of the remote people of the hills, not the access to modern education and medical facilities, not the access to water and sanitation and certainly not the right to development itself".

What we need to do is convert the hydropower projects in the state into agents of change and development through proper planning and management. Consistent monitoring of the implementation process is needed. Topography of the hill state doesn't allow it to have mass-scale industrialisation or to have any other growth-oriented model. Not having hydropower projects altogether shall have more disastrous effects on the overall development of the remote hills than having them. Just because implementation is bad, it cannot be concluded that the idea itself is not good.

CHAPTER I

INTRODUCTION

Development is as perennial as earth itself. It was happening even when people were not start measuring it in time and space. Since that time, the development of human civilisations started being measured, and then perhaps we realised that our resources are not unlimited. So we began to be conscious about the source of our resources (i.e. nature).

Development having a transanthropocentric approach is sustainable development. Generally understood, the idea of environmental and ecological protection, added with the principles of economic and social development, transforms into the concept of sustainable development. The figure below shows the idea of sustainable development and its components.

Sustainable Development Components

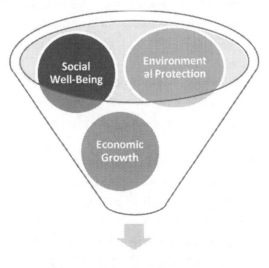

Sustainable Development

Figure 1

Sustainable development is possible when the equality- and equity-based distribution of resources is ensured, when social well-being is prioritised in the collective efforts of a society, and when ecology and environmental protection is made a preliminary requirement or any basic ingredient of all growth models. Sustainable development is about ensuring a fine balance amongst social upliftment, economic growth, and environmental protection. Contemporary jurisprudence has very recently recognised the role of social and economic factors in the overall developmental process. Hitherto sustainable development jurisprudence has always been predominated with the ideas of environmental and ecological protection.

Chanakya in *Arthashastra* (treatise of politics and statecraft) provides various duties of the king and subjects towards nature. King Ashoka in the Fifth Pillar Edict has instructed his subjects to respect Mother Nature and provided various measures to live in harmony with the environment. With the advent of the Industrial Revolution in Britain, trouble started. Resource consumption was at its height, and the rulers of colonies looked around the world with similar intentions, which was one of the major reasons for colonial imperialism. Then they realised that the time has come for some serious thinking. After the two wars (World Wars I and II) of great greed and insanity, the institution of the concept of sustainable development finally began.

'Environment' may connote different meanings in different contexts. As it is commonly understood, the environment consists of the surroundings: the air, water, soil, and, to be more general, our habitat. Broadly, we can divide the environment into two specific concepts: one is the natural environment, and the other is a built environment. Natural environment consists of all living and nonliving things that occur naturally on earth; and a built environment includes buildings, roads, parks, gardens, powerhouses, dams, and other man-made things. As defined in section 2 (a) of the Environment (Protection) Act of 1986, the term 'environment' means to 'include water, air and land and the inter-relationships which exist among and in between water, air and land, human beings and other living creatures, plants, micro-organisms and property'.[1]

The concept of sustainable development is all about the harmonious coexistence of the natural environment with a man-made environment.

---

[1]   Section 2 (a) of the Environment (Protection) Act, 1986.

Development must be such which can be sustained by future generations. We cannot grow haphazardly; we have to develop equitably. The elements of intergenerational equity and a transanthropocentric approach must be given real consideration while chalking out any developmental activity.

Humanity's demand for the planet's resources has more than doubled over the past century as a result of population growth and increasing per capita consumption. The latter half of the twentieth century witnessed a phenomenal increase in population; and industry led to the urbanisation of people, which has been supplemented by an increase in food production, energy usage, and economic activities.

As the world has become more industrialised, there have been increasing pressures on the environment and the earth's resources that have resulted in harmful emissions and waste, which have had local, regional, and global impacts. At the local level, these include urban air pollution, contamination of soils and rivers, and land degradation; regionally, acid rain and water and coastal zone contamination; and globally, climate change, ozone-layer depletion, loss of biodiversity, transboundary movement of hazardous wastes, and increased land-based marine pollution. The challenges for a sustainable environment are elucidated in table 1 below.

Table 1. Challenges for a Sustainable Environment

Regional	Global
Urban air pollution	Climate change
Noise pollution	Threat for polar regions
Rapid soil erosion	Ozone-layer depletion
Contamination of rivers, ponds, and other bodies of water	Loss of biodiversity
Population explosion	Transboundary movement of hazardous wastes, marine pollution
Poverty and corruption	Terrorism

The issues confronting the development process today are to achieve desired development for economic or social reasons on one hand and to safeguard the environment and maintain good-quality living conditions on the other. The haphazard and uncontrolled developmental activities are the primary reason for the overuse of natural resources, congestion, incompatible land use, and poor living conditions. The problems of habitat pollution are becoming complex and are creating a high-risk environment.

Sustainable development is the only answer the present generation can give to future generations when asked about the use of earth's resources. As far as the legal arena is concerned, international law on sustainable development is not more than a soft law in the form of various treaties and conventions. Sustainability principles are yet to permeate into the domestic legislations of almost all countries of the world. In India, sustainability facets of legislations are yet to be legislated. Being one of the largest populated countries on the planet, balancing the growing demands of the population with sustainable development principles will be another challenge for the Indian lawmakers. In the absence of legislative enactments on this new area, Indian courts have done a remarkable job in this field. Applying common law principles while deciding public interest litigation, the Supreme Court of India as well as its high courts empowered with constitutional authority have presented a unique fusion of environmental, social, and economic growth concerns. Interpreting a healthy and sustainable environment as a part of article 21 (right to life), Indian courts have done much service to the idea of sustainable development.

India has enacted some landmark legislations in the recent past, ensuring social well-being and economic security. These include the Mahatma Gandhi National Rural Employment Guarantee Act 2005, the National Food Security Act 2013, and the Right to Education Act 2009 for its billion-plus population (most of them are below the poverty line by global standards). Such beneficial legislations are necessary for balancing economic growth with the social and economic well-being of its weaker sections to ensure sustainable development for a society.

Literally, sustainable development has been defined by *Black's Law Dictionary* as 'the use of natural resources in a manner that can be maintained and supported over time, taking into account the needs of future generations'.[2]

---

[2] *Black's Law Dictionary*, 10th edition, Thomson Reuters, 2014, p. 1676.

Oxford English Dictionary defines sustainable development as: 'Conserving an ecological balance by avoiding depletion of natural resources'.[3]

'Development' has been defined differently every time depending on the time of the study. A very specific purpose of this research work is to find connotations of development and the contours of sustainable development presently in the state of Uttarakhand. An empirical study has been conducted for this purpose, which also includes the survey of the residents of the Uttarakhand, and the views of the people involved in the survey have been incorporated into relevant portions of the study. The issue to be answered through this study is 'right to development versus right to environment'. In a state like Uttarakhand, where even basic medical and educational facilities are a distant dream, sustainable development is in a different context from rest of the world. Is this remote state and its more remote people entitled to a head start in this so-called globalised and growth-oriented world?

The Himalayan state is credited with giving birth to the modern Indian environmental movement. On the 27 March 1973, a group of peasants in a remote Himalayan village stopped a group of loggers from felling a patch of trees. Thus, the Chipko movement was born and, through it, the modern Indian environmental movement itself.[4]

In the 1980s and 1990s, the finest minds in the environmental movement sought to marry science with sustainability. They sought to design and implement forest, energy, water, and transportation policies that would augment economic productivity and human welfare without causing stress on the environment. They acted on the knowledge that, unlike the West, India did not have colonies whose resources it could draw upon in its own industrial revolution.[5]

The new state of Uttaranchal, now renamed as Uttarakhand, was formed under article 3 of the Constitution of India by an act of parliament known as the Uttar Pradesh Reorganization Act 2000 (hereinafter referred to as

---

[3]   *Oxford Dictionary of English*, 3rd edition, Oxford University Press, 2010, p. 1793.

[4]   See Ramchandra Guha, 'The Past and Present of Indian Environmentalism', *The Hindu*, 27 March 2013; article available at www.thehindu.com/opinion, last visited on 27 March 2013.

[5]   Ibid.

'Reorganization Act'). The new state of Uttarakhand came into existence on the 'appointed day', which is 9 November 2000. The Reorganization Act of 2000 does not contain any preamble for any specific purpose of the creation of the new state; however, the new state was created for the specific reason of the development of the hilly regions hitherto considered backward and less developed of the erstwhile state of Uttar Pradesh.

Since the creation of the new state, many development initiatives have been taken by the people of the state. Uttarakhand is a very rich state in terms of water resources and forests. Hydropower has been one of the key areas in which considerable development has been done by the state. The most successful hydropower project of the State is the Tehri Hydro Power Project. A preliminary investigation of the Tehri Dam was done in 1961 with a 600 MW capacity power plant for which technical and financial assistance was to be provided by the then USSR. With the change of the political circumstances of the supporting nation, India itself had to take over the project completely, and the project was placed under the direction of the Irrigation Department of the then state of Uttar Pradesh. In 1988, the Tehri Hydro Development Corporation was formed to manage the dam, with 75 per cent of the funding by the central government and 25 per cent by the state government. Tehri Dam, having a height of 261 metres, is claimed to be the eighth tallest hydropower dam in the world.

Tehri Dam may be taken as a good example of sustainable development efforts, balancing ecology and development in the state. However, many environmentalists have time and again challenged the sustainability of the project. Issues related to the catchment area development, command area development, and religious sensibility of the Bhagirathi River were raised during its completion and implementation.

The construction and final commissioning of the Tehri Dam also addressing all the sustainability issues have been a major success story of the state and its people.

Uttarakhand is a young state with rapid economic growth, and it has made constant efforts to incorporate sustainable development jurisprudence into its policy initiatives. Sustainable development tenets are all the more important for the state of Uttarakhand, as most of the people here are dependent on their natural habitat, which is evident from the fact that over three-fourths of the total population is dependent on agriculture for its livelihood. The state has over fifteen important rivers and over a dozen glaciers in its land, thus also a valuable freshwater reserve. About 200 large- and medium-sized hydropower projects are in operational or various stages of development; therefore, hydroelectricity is credited as the prime source of capital for the local economy. Maintaining the 'high precautionary approach' towards sustainability of the environment and ecology-comprehensive environment-impact assessments (EIAs) are a necessary part of the hydropower projects of the state.

Speaking at the Uttarakhand Sustainable Development Summit (USDS) in 2008, organised by the government of Uttarakhand and the Energy and Resources Institute (TERI) in Dehradun, the then chief minister, Major General B. C. Khanduri, stated, 'The State needs a people friendly and rural oriented model of development that does not disrupt the life of masses and the livelihoods of the rural population, but helps them grow in every aspect of life, be it economic development or ecological development or management of natural resources.'[6]

Incorporating natural resource–friendly policies and practices is important for the state, as it is very vulnerable to the impact of climate change despite its rich natural resource heritage. A sustainability audit is the need of the hour for all the new and old hydropower projects of the state. As a new state, Uttarakhand has a chance to lay a blueprint of its growth. Because of its very rich natural environment, this state needs policies that ensures its sustainable development.

Uttarakhand has an estimated hydropower potential of approximately 20,000 MW; only about 3,124 MW has been harnessed so far.[7] The position with regard to the sources of energy supply and energy consumption based on use for the 2008–2009 was assessed by the Comptroller and Auditor General of India (CAG) while doing performance audit on hydropower development

---

[6] See http://news.oneindia.in/2008/06/19/khanduri-sustainable-development-natural-resource-management-uttarakhand-1213878600.html.

[7] See Performance Audit Report prepared by the Comptroller and Auditor General of India. Report available online at http://saiindia.gov.in/english/home/Our_Products/Audit_Report/Government_Wise/state_audit/recent_reports/Uttarakhand/2009/performance_Audit/performance_Audit_Uttarakhand_2009/pa_chap1.pdf, last visited on 13 July 2013.

through private sector participation in the state of Uttarakhand. Sources of energy were identified by the CAG as follows:

Sources of Energy Identified by the CAG

	Sources of Energy in the State of Uttarakhand (in million units [MUs])		
1.	Own Sources	4419.08 MUs	52 %
2.	Central Pool	3379.57 MUs	39%
3.	Other Sources	770.22 MUs	9%

Table 2[8]

It is very clear from the above data that the state of Uttarakhand is way behind in its ambition of becoming an energy-surplus state. The state is able to meet only 52 per cent of its power needs from its own resources. Looking at the grim state of affairs of the power production and distribution of energy in the state, the state government has from time to time emphasised the construction of hydroelectricity projects in the state. Apart from the production pattern, a consumption pattern has also been identified by the CAG as follows:

Consumption of Energy Identified by the CAG

	Consumption of Energy in the State of Uttarakhand Based on 2008–2009 Data (in million units [MUs])		
1.	Domestic	1222.22 MUs	22%
2.	Commercial	763.92 MUs	14%
3.	Irrigation	266.01 MUs	5%
4.	Industrial	2980.84 MUs	54%
5.	Others	260.76 MUs	5%

Table 3[9]

---

[8] Ibid.
[9] Ibid.

Hydropower projects are similar in nature to high dams with large generation capacity and small run-of-the-river projects. Looking into the sustainability and community-friendly aspects, the state of Uttarakhand has encouraged small run-of-the-river projects. The state of Uttarakhand framed a policy for the small hydropower projects up to the capacity of 25 MW. Defining the scope for small hydropower development in the state, it said, 'Uttaranchal has a hydropower potential of the order of 20236 MW against which only about 1407 MW has been harnessed so far. The Government of Uttaranchal has decided to encourage generation of power through small hydropower sources of energy, and has framed a policy so that the development of this sector serves as an engine to achieve the objective of promoting the all-round development of the region.'[10]

In the year 2001, the state of Uttarakhand created a specialised state-operated company called Uttarakhand Jal Vidyut Nigam Ltd. (UJVNL). UJVNL is a wholly owned corporation of the government of Uttarakhand set up for the management of hydropower generation at existing power stations and for the development and promotion of new hydro projects with the purpose of harnessing the known and yet-to-be-known hydropower resources of the state.[11]

Due to the hilly terrain of the state, it was found by the power infrastructure laying agencies that all the areas must be linked to the grid. A large part of the state land is made up of forests and reserve parks like Corbett National Park and Nanda Devi Wildlife Reserve, and this added to the problem of linking electricity distribution lines to the transmission lines or the grid. To tackle this problem, policymakers found micro power production as a viable solution in the remote and rural areas. For that, the Uttarakhand Renewable Energy Development Agency (UREDA) was created for the decentralised production and supply of power in the remote villages not connected to the grid either due to their remoteness or because of the scattered nature of the villages throughout the mountainous areas of the state. Micro hydro projects are in the nature of stand-alone projects and are built for the specific needs of a local area.

The Himalayan state tackled this problem in a very unique way. It started Decentralised Distributed Generation (DDG) through micro and

---

[10]   See http://www.ireda.gov.in.
[11]   See http://www.uttarakhandjalvidyut.com.

mini hydro projects (MHPs), which are suitable and the best way to provide electricity facilities to the forest fringe and scattered villages. In the absence of national and state grid lines in these remote villages, a large number of MHPs are being commissioned by the state for stand-alone generation and supply of electricity. UREDA, which is a nodal agency for this purpose, has commissioned a large number of MHPs in the remote areas of the state where the national or state grid cannot be extended. A total of forty-one MHPs with a total capacity of 3.960 MW have been installed in the remote villages of Uttarakhand to date, and another eighteen MHPs with a total capacity of 1.965 MW are under implementation.

The tables below amply describe the potential of as well as the need for micro hydropower projects in the state of Uttarakhand. Because of its geographical conditions, this state needs more and more micro power generation. Remote areas in hills and scattered population settlements mandated the policymakers in the state to generate electricity more and more through micro hydro projects and also ensure a decentralised distribution of power. Instead of the grid supply, which is very well effective in large cities and in places having concentrated population, decentralised generation and distribution are more suitable to the needs of the Himalayan state. MHPs commissioned during the 2010–2011 and MHPs under construction in the state are stated in tables 4 and 5, respectively.

Micro Hydro Projects Commissioned in the State

MHPs Commissioned during 2010–2011					
Sl.	District	Project	Capacity (KW)	Electrified	
				Nos. of Villages	Nos. of Hamlets
1	Tehri	Jakhana	100	3	4
2	Chamoli	Bank	100	5	3
3	Chamoli	Gamsali-Bampa	50	2	-
4	Bageshwar	Lamabagar	200	4	4
5	Bageshwar	Borbalada	25	1	2

6	Uttarkaski	Taluka	25	-	1
	Total		500	15	14

Table 4[12]

After looking at the success of the above-mentioned micro hydro projects, the state government encouraged the increase of electricity generation through this model. The table below shows such encouragement to the micro hydro projects in the state. Villages and hamlets of the villages shall be the direct beneficiaries of this idea.

Micro Hydro Projects Under Construction in the State

Sl.	District	Project	Capacity (KW)	To be Electrified	
				Nos. of Villages	Nos. of Hamlets
1	Almora	Tarula	100	5	3
2	Bageshwar	Lamchula	50	2	2
3	Bageshwar	Gogina-II	50	3	-
4	Bageshwar	Wachham	500	2	8
5	Pauri	Gaudi Chida	250	Grid Feeding	
6	Chamoli	Hafla	200	Grid Feeding	
7	Chamoli	Nigolgad	100	Grid Feeding	
8	Uttarkashi	Khapugad	40	1	-
9	Tehri	Pinswad	50	2	-
10	Tehri	Kotijhala	200	4	1
11	Uttarkashi	Chiludgad	100	4	-

---

[12] Department of Renewable Energy: Government of Uttarakhand; last updated on 18 March 2013, data available online at http://ureda.uk.gov.in/pages/display/131-micro-hydro-projects.

12	Pithoragarh	Rotan	50	3	2
13	Pithoragarh	Duktu	25	2	-
14	Pithoragarh	Nagling	50	3	-
15	Pithoragarh	Sela	50	1	-
16	Pithoragarh	Kutty	50	1	-
17	Pithoragarh	Napalchu	50	2	-
18	Pithoragarh	Bundi	50	1	-
19	Pithoragarh	Rongkong	50	1	-
20	Rudraprayag	Kedarnath II	200	1	Kedarnath Dham
	Total		2215	38	16

Table 5[13]

The above data amply confirms the success of the micro hydro projects in the State. Apart from the isolated villages, another very important achievement reached through these micro hydro projects is the supply of electricity to the shrines. Badrinath Shrine, Kedarnath Shrine, Yamunotri Shrine, Gangotri Shrine, Hemkund Shrine, Jageshwar Temples, etc., are religious places of national importance; due to these, Uttarakhand has a special place in the religious and mythological maps of the country. Four religious shrines of utmost importance to Hindus are in the state. UREDA has successfully implemented the micro hydro projects in the four shrines; as a result, these shrines now no longer depend on the power supply from the grid. All the power to these shrines comes from the micro hydro projects installed locally.

[13]   Ibid.

Decentralised Generation and Distribution to the Shrines

Self-Sustaining Green Power Supply through MHP Model

Sl.	Shrine	Type	Capacity	Agency
1.	Kedarnath Shrine	MHP	100 KW	UREDA
2.	Yamunotri Shrine	MHP	2 x100 KW	UREDA
3.	Gangotri Shrine	MHP	3x 50 KW	UREDA
4.	Hemkund Sahib	MHP	2x 50 KW	UREDA

Table 6[14]

The above-mentioned model indicates that the concept of micro hydro projects for remote area electrification in the state of Uttarakhand is completely sustainable as well as having minimal or no impact on the surrounding natural habitat. It is a self-sustaining green power supply model possible only through the concept of micro hydro projects.

---

[14] Data based on calculations of the Uttarakhand Renewable Energy Development Agency under Department of Renewable Energy, government of Uttarakhand, available at http://ureda.uk.gov.in/pages/display/55-shrine-electrification.

CHAPTER II

PRINCIPLES OF SUSTAINABLE DEVELOPMENT

A special concern for the environment, economy, and society while balancing economic growth and social development is generally called the principle of sustainable development. Each and every ecosystem in which humans interact for development has its carrying capacity. The principle of sustainable development mandates that while striving for economic growth and social development, caution should be taken in the carrying capacity of the ecosystem. Major sustainable development principles are listed in the figure below.

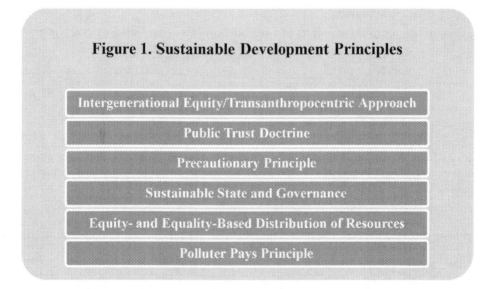

Figure 1. Sustainable Development Principles

Intergenerational Equity/Transanthropocentric Approach

Public Trust Doctrine

Precautionary Principle

Sustainable State and Governance

Equity- and Equality-Based Distribution of Resources

Polluter Pays Principle

Intergenerational Equity

Intergenerational equity simply implies the duty of the present generation towards future generations in which the present generation is obliged to take care of natural resources and ecology so that all future generations shall also have an equal chance of enjoying Mother Nature and the right to life. The present generation has an obligation to use earth's resources in a manner that to sustains its utility for the next generation and beyond. The Brundtland Commission[15] clearly emphasised the importance of the concept of intergenerational equity. It says that 'we borrow environmental capital from future generations with no intention or prospect of repaying . . . We act as we do because we can get away with it: future generations do not vote; they have no political or financial power; they cannot challenge our decisions'.[16] Self-control and self-regulation are the blueprints on which the whole concept of intergenerational equity is premised.

A transanthropocentric approach of development is essential for achieving sustainability in growth and human settlements on earth. This report has very famously incorporated the duty of present generations towards future generations in the following words: 'Development that meets the needs of the present without compromising the ability of future generations to meet their own needs.'[17]

Prof. Edith Brown Weiss in her seminal paper 'The Planetary Trust: Conservation and Intergenerational Equity'[18] described the idea of intergenerational trust as follows: 'This planetary trust obligates each generation to preserve the diversity of the resource base and to pass the planet to future generations in no worse condition than it receives it. Thus, the present generation serves both as a trustee for future generations and as a beneficiary of the trust.'[19] We have a fiduciary role to play towards future generations. With the present rate in the growth of the human population compared with resource depletion, we shall have more people to service with lesser earth resources in hand. So an equitable distribution of natural resources amongst 'present and future people' is the needed.

---

[15] Report of the World Commission on Environment and Development, United Nations, 1987; available at http://worldinbalance.net/pdf/ 1987-brundtland.pdf.

[16] Ibid.

[17] Ibid.

[18] Prof. Edith Brown Weiss, 'The Planetary Trust: Conservation and Intergenerational Equity', *Ecology Law Quarterly*, vol. 11, no. 4, Georgetown Law Faculty Publications, 2010; available at http://scholarship.law.georgetown.edu/facpub/334/.

[19] Id. at p. 499.

A transhuman-centric approach for the use and preservation of environmental values can provide a solution to the haphazard growth model. A growth devoid of sustainability concerns is not sustainable. We have to take care that what we build can also serve future generations.

Public Trust Doctrine

The origins of the public trust doctrine can be traced back to Roman law concepts of common property. Under Roman jurisprudence, the air, the waters, and the forests were public property and could not be owned by private persons. The purpose of such restrictions on private ownership of common resources was to make natural resources good for the public at large. Roman law recognised the public trust doctrine whereby common properties such as rivers, seashores, forests, and the air were held by the government in trust for free use for all: 'These resources were either owned by no one (*res nullious*) or by everyone in common (*res communious*).'[20] The facets of the public trust doctrine have been provided in figure 2 below.

Figure 2. Facets of Public Trust Doctrine

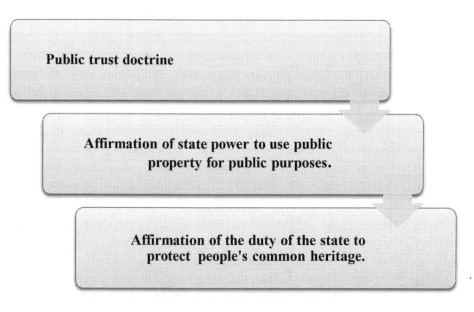

Public trust doctrine

Affirmation of state power to use public property for public purposes.

Affirmation of the duty of the state to protect people's common heritage.

---

[20] See Justice Madan B. Lokur, 'Environmental Law: Its Development and Jurisprudence' lecture available at http://awsassets.wwfindia.org/.

All natural goods are held by the state in public trust for their equitable distribution. Private ownership of natural resources can lead to undue deprivation of such resources for a large section of society. Therefore, the modern state is mandated to hold them in public trust and ensure their equal distribution for a sustainable social structure. 'The public trust doctrine is more than an affirmation of State power to use public property for public purposes. It is an affirmation of the duty of the State to protect the people's common heritage of streams, lakes, marshlands and tidelands, surrendering the right only in those rare cases when the abandonment of the right is consistent with the purposes of the trust.'[21]

The modern tenets of public trust were evolved in *Illinois Central Railroad Co. v. People of the State of Illinois*.[22] In this early case, the Supreme Court of United States differentiated the nature of the title of the state in the land intended to be used for public good from the land intended for sale or other commercial purposes. The U.S. Supreme Court considered whether the state could abdicate its general control over the submerged land. In the year 1869, the Illinois legislature made a substantial grant of submerged land—a strip along the shores of Lake Michigan extending one mile out from the shoreline—to the Illinois Central Railroad. This was repealed in 1869. The state of Illinois sued to quit title. The Supreme Court, while accepting the stand of the state of Illinois, held that the title of the state in the land in dispute was a title different in character from that which the State held in lands intended for sale. It was different from the title which the United States held in public lands which were open to preemption and sale. It was a title held in trust—for the people of the state that they may enjoy the navigation of the water, carry on commerce over them, and have the liberty of fishing therein free from obstruction or interference of private parties. The abdication of the general control of the state over lands in dispute was not consistent with the exercise of the trust which required the government of the state to preserve such waters for the use of the public.[23]

---

[21] Dr. Geir B. Asheim, 'Intergenerational Equity', *Annual Review of Economics*, vol. 2, September 2010, University of Oslo, 2010; available at http://www.annualreviews.org/doi/abs/10.1146/annurev.economics.102308.124440.

[22] 146 (1892) U.S. 387.

[23] Ibid.

In *National Audubon Society v. Superior Court of Alpine County*,[24] the Supreme Court of California considered whether a permit can be granted to the Department of Water and Power of the city of Los Angeles to appropriate water of four of the five streams flowing into Mono Lake, which is the second largest lake in California. Some environmentalists, using the public trust doctrine, brought a lawsuit against Los Angeles's water diversion. The Supreme Court of California explained the concept of the public trust doctrine in the following words: 'By the law of nature these things are common to mankind—the air, running water, the sea and consequently the shores of the sea. From this origin in Roman law, the English common law evolved the concept of the public trust, under which the sovereign owns "all of its navigable waterways and the lands lying beneath them as trustee of a public trust for the benefit of the people".'

While dealing with the State's power as a trustee of public property, the Court observed the following: 'Thus, the public trust is more than an affirmation of State power to use public property for public purposes. It is an affirmation of the duty of the State to protect the people's common heritage of streams, lakes, marshlands and tidelands, surrendering that right of protection only in rare cases when the abandonment of that right is consistent with the purposes of the trust . . .'

The court recorded its conclusion in the following words: 'The State has an affirmative duty to take the public trust into account in the planning and allocation of water resources, and to protect public trust uses whenever feasible. Just as the history of this State shows that appropriation may be necessary for efficient use of water despite unavoidable harm to public trust values, it demonstrates that an appropriative water rights system administered without consideration of the public trust may cause unnecessary and unjustified harm to trust interests. As a matter of practical necessity the State may have to approve appropriations despite foreseeable harm to public trust uses. In so doing, however, the State must bear in mind its duty as trustee to consider the effect of the taking on the public trust [see *United Plainsmen v. ND State Water Cons. Conum'n*, 247 NW 2d 457 (ND 1976) at pp. 462–463], and to preserve, so far as consistent with the public interest, the uses protected by the trust.'[25]

---

[24] 33 Cal. 3d 419.

[25] Ibid.

The Hon'ble Supreme Court of India has also held the doctrine of public trust as part of Indian jurisprudence on sustainable development in the case of *M. C. Mehta v. Kamal Nath.*[26] In this landmark case, Justice Kuldip Singh, writing for himself and for Justice S. Saghir Ahmed, held the following: 'The source of modern public trust law is found in a concept that received much attention in Roman and English law—the nature of property rights in rivers, the sea, and the seashore. That history has been given considerable attention in the legal literature need not be repeated in detail here. But two points should be emphasized, First, certain interests, such as navigation and fishing, were sought to be preserved for the benefit of the public; accordingly, property used for those purposes was distinguished from general public property which the sovereign could routinely grant to private owners. Second, while it was understood that in certain common properties— such as the seashore, highways, and running water—"perpetual use was dedicated to the public". It has never been clear whether the public had an enforceable right to prevent infringement of those interests. Although the state apparently did protect public uses, no evidence is available that public rights could be legally asserted against a recalcitrant government. The Public Trust Doctrine primarily rests on the principle that certain resources like air, sea, waters and the forests have such a great importance to the people as a whole that it would be wholly unjustified to make them a subject of private ownership. The said resources being a gift of nature, they should be made freely available to everyone irrespective of the status in life. The doctrine enjoins upon the government to protect the resources for the enjoyment of the general public rather than to permit their use for private ownership or commercial purposes. Our legal system—based on English Common Law— includes the public trust doctrine as part of its jurisprudence. The State is the trustee of all natural resources which are by nature meant for public use and enjoyment. Public at large is the beneficiary of the seashore, running waters, air, forests and ecologically fragile lands. The State as a trustee is under a legal duty to protect the natural resources. These resources meant for public use cannot be converted into private ownership.'[27]

Figure 3 below states the components of state trusteeship. The state trusteeship includes the right of first and beneficial use of forest land and

---

[26]   1997 (1) SCC 388.

[27]   Ibid.

produce under its territory. The idea of giving all waters under the trusteeship of the state is to preserve the bodies of water and make them good for public use. As shown in the figure below, air and ecologically fragile lands have also been put under the state trusteeship to ensure pollution-free air to the people. Ecologically fragile lands need special care and protection from individual greed; hence, they can be preserved only while under state trusteeship. Under the idea of state trusteeship, the state is mandated to preserve and protect all the above-mentioned natural public goods.

Figure 3. Components of State Trusteeship

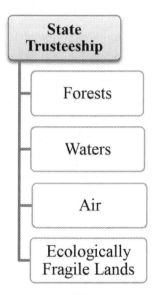

In *Jamshed Hormusji Wadia v. Board of Trustee, Port of Mumbai*,[28] the Supreme Court of India held that the state's actions and the actions of its agencies/instrumentalities must be for the public good, achieving the objects for which they exist and should not be arbitrary or capricious. In the field of contracts, the state and its instrumentalities should design their activities in a manner which would ensure competition and nondiscrimination. They can augment their resources, but the objective should be to serve the public cause and to do public good by resorting to fair and reasonable methods.

---

[28] 2002 (3) SCC 214.

In the *Fomento Resorts and Hotels Limited* case, the court referred to the article of Prof. Joseph L. Sax and made the following observations: 'The public trust doctrine enjoins upon the Government to protect the resources for the enjoyment of the general public rather than to permit their use for private ownership or commercial purposes. This doctrine puts an implicit embargo on the right of the State to transfer public properties to private party if such transfer affects public interest, mandates affirmative State action for effective management of natural resources and empowers the citizens to question ineffective management thereof. The heart of the public trust doctrine is that it imposes limits and obligations upon government agencies and their administrators on behalf of all the people and especially future generations. For example, renewable and non-renewable resources, associated uses, ecological values or objects in which the public has a special interest (i.e. public lands, waters, etc.) are held subject to the duty of the State not to impair such resources, uses or values, even if private interests are involved. The same obligations apply to managers of forests, monuments, parks, the public domain and other public assets. Professor Joseph L. Sax in his classic article, "The Public Trust Doctrine in Natural Resources Law: Effective Judicial Intervention" (1970), indicates that the public trust doctrine, of all concepts known to law, constitutes the best practical and philosophical premise and legal tool for protecting public rights and for protecting and managing resources, ecological values or objects held in trust. The public trust doctrine is a tool for exerting long-established public rights over short-term public rights and private gain. Today every person exercising his or her right to use the air, water, or land and associated natural ecosystems has the obligation to secure for the rest of us the right to live or otherwise use that same resource or property for the long-term and enjoyment by future generations. To say it another way, a landowner or lessee and a water right holder has an obligation to use such resources in a manner as not to impair or diminish the people's rights and the people's long-term interest in that property or resource, including down slope lands, waters and resources.'[29]

In a very landmark judgement delivered by the constitution bench of the Hon'ble Supreme Court of India—comprising Justice Jagdish Singh Khehar, Justice S. H. Kapadia, Justice D. K. Jain, Justice Dipak Misra, and Justice Ranjan Gogoi—while exercising its advisory jurisdiction in the case

---

[29]   Ibid.

of In Re: Special Reference No. 1 of 2012,[30] it held the following: 'As far as "trusteeship" is concerned, there is no cavil that the State holds all natural resources as a trustee of the public and must deal with them in a manner that is consistent with the nature of such a trust.'[31]

Precautionary Principle

Principle 15 of the Rio Declaration of 1992[32] declares, 'Where there are threats of serious or irreversible environmental damage, lack of full scientific certainty should not be used as a reason for postponing measures to prevent environmental degradation.' International Law Association, New Delhi Declaration 2002,[33] postulates a much wider definition of the precautionary principle. Traditionally, the precautionary principle was deemed to be related only to environmental safety and standards. After the New Delhi Declaration, the scope of precautionary approach has widened. It declares the principle of precautionary approach as follows: 'The principle of the precautionary approach to human health, natural resources and ecosystems. A precautionary approach is central to sustainable development in that it commits States, international organizations and the civil society, particularly the scientific and business communities, to avoid human activity which may cause significant harm to human health, natural resources or ecosystems, including in the light of scientific uncertainty.'[34] Sustainable development requires that a precautionary approach with regard to human health, environmental protection, and sustainable utilisation of natural resources should include the following:

    a. accountability for harm caused (including, where appropriate, state responsibility)

---

[30]   2012 (10) SCC 352.

[31]   Ibid.

[32]   See Principle 15, Rio Declaration on Environment and Development, United Nations Conference on Environment and Development, Rio De Janeiro, 1992; available athttp://www.unep.org/Documents.Multilingual/Default.Print.asp?documentid=78&articleid=1163.

[33]   See Report of the Seventieth Conference, International Law Association, New Delhi, 2002; available at http://www.ila-hq.org/en/publications/order-reports.cfm.

[34]   Ibid. See paragraph no. 4.1.

b.   planning based on clear criteria and well-defined goals

c.   consideration in an environmental impact assessment of all possible means to achieve an objective (including, in certain instances, not proceeding with an envisaged activity)

d.   in respect to activities that may cause serious long-term or irreversible harm, establishing an appropriate burden of proof on the person or persons carrying out (or intending to carry out) the activity[35]

Decision-making processes should always endorse a precautionary approach to risk management and in particular should include the adoption of appropriate precautionary measures.[36] Precautionary measures should be based on up-to-date and independent scientific judgement and be transparent. They should not result in economic protectionism. Transparent structures that involve all interested parties, including nonstate actors, in the consultation process should be established. Appropriate review by a judicial or administrative body should be available.[37]

However, a large part of the traditional precautionary principle still revolves around basic environment laws. In the matter of *A. P. Pollution Control Board v. Prof. M. V. Nayudu (Retd.) and Others*,[38] a division bench of the Supreme Court of India defined the traditional concept of precautionary principle and its applicability in the Indian sustainable development law jurisprudence.

The court defined it as follows: 'The Precautionary Principle replaces the Assimilative Capacity Principle: A basic shift in the approach to environmental protection occurred initially between 1972 and 1982. Earlier the Concept was based on the "assimilative capacity" rule as revealed from Principle 6 of the Stockholm Declaration of the U.N. Conference on Human Environment, 1972. The said principle assumed that science could provide policy-makers with the information and means necessary to avoid encroaching upon the capacity of the environment to assimilate impacts and it presumed that relevant technical expertise would be available when environmental harm was predicted and there would be sufficient time to

---

[35]   Ibid. See paragraph no. 4.2.

[36]   Ibid. See paragraph no. 4.3.

[37]   Ibid. See paragraph no. 4.4.

[38]   1999 (2) SCC 718.

act in order to avoid such harm. But in the 11th Principle of the U.N. General Assembly Resolution on World Charter for Nature, 1982, the emphasis shifted to the "Precautionary Principle", and this was reiterated in the Rio Conference of 1992 in its Principle 15 which reads as follows: Principle 15: In order to protect the environment, the precautionary approach shall be widely applied by States according to their capabilities. Where there are threats of serious or irreversible damage; lack of full scientific certainty shall not be used as a reason for proposing cost-effective measures to prevent environmental degradation.'[39]

Further elaborating the idea behind the development of the traditional precautionary principle, the court held, 'In other words, inadequacies of science is the real basis that has led to the Precautionary Principle of 1982. It is based on the theory that it is better to err on the side of caution and prevent environmental harm which may indeed become irreversible. The principle of precaution involves the anticipation of environmental harm and taking measures to avoid it or to choose the least environmentally harmful activity. It is based on scientific uncertainty. Environmental protection should not only aim at protecting health, property and economic interest but also protect the environment for its own sake. Precautionary duties must not only be triggered by the suspicion of concrete danger but also by (justified) concern or risk potential.'[40]

Polluter Pays Principle

This is also known as the *principle of extended producer responsibility.* With the advent of modern industrial revolution, the scheme of production in factories added the idea of externalising the waste. It caused pressure on the surrounding environment, and the need for the polluter pays principle arose. Those who damage the environment should bear the cost of such damage is the underlining idea of the polluter pays principle.

Defining the above-mentioned principle while delivering judgement in the matter of *Indian Council for Enviro-Legal Action v. Union of India and others,*[41] Justice Dalveer Bhandari for himself and Justice H. L. Dattu said,

---

[39]   Ibid.

[40]   Ibid.

[41]   2011 (8) SCC 161.

'The polluter pays principle demands that the financial costs of preventing or remedying damage caused by pollution should lie with the undertakings which cause the pollution, or produce the goods which cause the pollution. Under the principle it is not the role of government to meet the costs involved in either prevention of such damage, or in carrying out remedial action, because the effect of this would be to shift the financial burden of the pollution incident to the taxpayer. The "polluter pays" principle was promoted by the Organization for Economic Cooperation and Development (OECD) during the 1970s when there was great public interest in environmental issues. During this time there were demands on government and other institutions to introduce policies and mechanisms for the protection of the environment and the public from the threats posed by pollution in a modern industrialized society.'[42]

In the case of *M. C. Mehta and Another v. Union of India and Others*,[43] Justice P. N. Bhagwati writing for a constitution bench consisting of Justice G. L. Oza, Justice K. N. Singh, Justice M. M. Dutt, and Justice Ranganath Misra discussed the need for the development of the polluter pays principle in Indian sustainable development jurisprudence. The bench held the following: 'We must also deal with one other question which was seriously debated before us and that question is as to what is the measure of liability of an enterprise which is engaged in a hazardous or inherently dangerous industry, if by reason of an accident occurring in such industry, persons die or are injured. Does the rule in *Rylands v. Fletcher* apply or is there any other principle on which the liability can be determined? The rule in *Rylands v. Fletcher* was evolved in the year 1866 and it provides that a person who for his own purposes brings on to his land and collects and keeps there anything likely to do mischief if it escapes must keep it at his peril and, if he fails to do so, is prima facie liable for the damage which is the natural consequence of its escape. The liability under this rule is strict and it is no defense that the thing escaped without that person's willful act, default or neglect or even that he had no knowledge of its existence. This rule laid down a principle of liability that if a person who brings on to his land and collects and keeps there anything likely to do harm and such thing escapes and does damage to another, he is liable to compensate for the damage caused. Of course,

---

[42]   Ibid.

[43]   1987 (1) SCC 395.

this rule applies only to non-natural user of the land and it does not apply to things naturally on the land or where the escape is due to an act of God and an act of a stranger or the default of the person injured or where the thing which escapes is present by the consent of the person injured or in certain cases where there is statutory authority. Considerable case law has developed in England as to what is natural and what is non-natural use of land and what are precisely the circumstances in which this rule may be displaced. But it is not necessary for us to consider these decisions laying down the parameters of this rule because in a modern industrial society with highly developed scientific knowledge and technology where hazardous or inherently dangerous industries are necessary to carry out part of the developmental programme, this rule evolved in the 19th Century at a time when all these developments of science and technology had not taken place cannot afford any guidance in evolving any standard of liability consistent with the constitutional norms and the needs of the present day economy and social structure. We need not feel inhibited by this rule which was evolved in this context of a totally different kind of economy. Law has to grow in order to satisfy the needs of the fast changing society and keep abreast with the economic developments taking place in the country. As new situations arise the law has to be evolved in order to meet the challenge of such new situations. Law cannot afford to remain static. We have to evolve new principles and lay down new norms which would adequately deal with the new problems which arise in a highly industrialized economy. We cannot allow our judicial thinking to be constricted by reference to the law as it prevails in England or for the matter of that in any other foreign country. We no longer need the crutches of a foreign legal order. We are certainly prepared to receive light from whatever source it comes but we have to build up our own jurisprudence and we cannot countenance an argument that merely because the law in England does not recognize the rule of strict and absolute liability in cases of hazardous or inherently dangerous activities or the rule as laid down in *Rylands v. Fletcher* as is developed in England recognizes certain limitations and exceptions. We in India must hold back our hands and not venture to evolve a new principle of liability since English courts have not done so. We have to develop our own law and if we find that it is necessary to construct a new principle of liability to deal with an unusual situation which has arisen and which is likely to arise in future on account of hazardous or inherently dangerous industries which are concomitant to an industrial economy, there is no reason why we should hesitate to evolve such principle of liability merely because it has not been so done in England. We are of the view that an enterprise which is engaged in a hazardous or inherently dangerous industry which poses a potential threat to the health and safety of the persons working in the factory and residing in the surrounding areas owes an absolute and non-derogable duty to the community to ensure that no harm results to anyone on account of the hazardous or inherently dangerous nature of the activity which it has undertaken. The enterprise must be held to be under an obligation to provide that the hazardous or inherently dangerous activity in which it is engaged must be conducted with the highest standards of safety and if any harm results on account of such activity, the enterprise must be absolutely liable to compensate for such harm and it should be no answer for the enterprise to say that it had taken all reasonable care and that the harm occurred without any negligence on its part. Since the persons harmed on account of the hazardous or inherently dangerous activity carried on by the enterprise would not be in position to isolate the process of operation from the hazardous preparation of substance or any other related element that caused the harm, the enterprise must be held strictly liable for causing such harm, as a part of the social cost for carrying on the hazardous or inherently dangerous activity."[44]

The court also pointed out that the measure of compensation in the kinds of previous cases must be correlated with the magnitude and capacity of the enterprise because such compensation must have a deterrent effect. The larger and more prosperous the enterprise, the greater the amount of compensation payable by it for the harm caused on account of an accident in the carrying out of hazardous or inherently dangerous activity.[45] The process of *environmental auditing* has to be implemented in the framework of industrial activities.

---

[44] Ibid.

[45] Justice P. N. Bhagwati, *My Tryst with Justice*, Universal Law Publishing Co. Pvt. Ltd., New Delhi, 2013, p. 118.

Equity- and Equality-Based Distribution of Resources

In *Hinch Lal Tiwari v. Kamala Devi and Others*,[46] the court held the following: 'It is important to notice that the material resources of the community like forests, tanks, ponds, hillock, mountain etc. are nature's bounty. They maintain delicate ecological balance. They need to be protected for a proper and healthy environment which enables people to enjoy a quality life which is the essence of the guaranteed right under Article 21 of the Constitution.'[47]

Economic growth can only be sustained when it is based on the principles of equity and equality. Common ownership of resources and their equitable distribution are fundamental tenets of the idea of the modern welfare state ensuring sustainable development. With the advent of modern ideas of equality and the infusion of sustainability jurisprudence in the law-making process, the Constitution of India (vide in its article 39[48]) also provides the policy of sustainable development to be adopted by the state. The table below connotes the idea of sustainable development in the Indian constitution.

Table 1. Sustainable Development Principles under Article 39 of the Constitution of India

Article 39	Certain principles of policy to be followed by the State The State shall, in particular, direct its policy towards securing-
(a)	that the citizens, men and women equally, have the right to an adequate means to livelihood;
(b)	that the ownership and control of the material resources of the community are so distributed as best to subserve the common good;
(c)	that the operation of the economic system does not result in the concentration of wealth and means of production to the common detriment;

---

[46] AIR 2001 SC 3215.

[47] Ibid.

[48] See article 39, the Constitution of India.

(d)	that there is equal pay for equal work for both men and women
(e)	that the health and strength of workers, men and women, and the tender age of children are not abused and that citizens are not forced by economic necessity to enter avocations unsuited to their age or strength;
(f)	that children are given opportunities and facilities to develop in a healthy manner and in conditions of freedom and dignity and that childhood and youth are protected against exploitation and against moral and material abandonment

The Supreme Court of India in a much seminal decision in *Centre for Public Interest Litigation and Others v. Union of India and Others*[49] defined the resources of the country. It said, 'At the outset, we consider it proper to observe that even though there is no universally accepted definition of natural resources, they are generally understood as elements having intrinsic utility to mankind. They may be renewable or nonrenewable. They are thought of as the individual elements of the natural environment that provide economic and social services to human society and are considered valuable in their relatively unmodified, natural, form. A natural resource's value rests in the amount of the material available and the demand for it. The latter is determined by its usefulness to production. Natural resources belong to the people but the State legally owns them on behalf of its people and from that point of view natural resources are considered as national assets, more so because the State benefits immensely from their value. The State is empowered to distribute natural resources. However, as they constitute public property/national asset, while distributing natural resources, the State is bound to act in consonance with the principles of equality and public trust and ensure that no action is taken which may be detrimental to public interest. Like any other State action, constitutionalism must be reflected at every stage of the distribution of natural resources. In Article 39(b) of the Constitution it has been provided that the ownership and control of the material resources of the community should be

---

[49] 2012 (3) SCC 1.

so distributed so as to best sub-serve the common good, but no comprehensive legislation has been enacted to generally define natural resources and a framework for their protection. of course, environment laws enacted by Parliament and State legislatures deal with specific natural resources, i.e., Forest, Air, Water, Costal Zones, etc. The ownership regime relating to natural resources can also be ascertained from international conventions and customary international law, common law and national constitutions. In international law, it rests upon the concept of sovereignty and seeks to respect the principle of permanent sovereignty (of peoples and nations) over (their) natural resources as asserted in the 17th Session of the United Nations General Assembly and then affirmed as a customary international norm by the International Court of Justice in the case opposing the Democratic Republic of Congo to Uganda. Common Law recognizes States as having the authority to protect natural resources insofar as the resources are within the interests of the general public. The State is deemed to have a proprietary interest in natural resources and must act as guardian and trustee in relation to the same. Constitutions across the world focus on establishing natural resources as owned by, and for the benefit of, the country. In most instances where constitutions specifically address ownership of natural resources, the Sovereign State, or, as it is more commonly expressed, "the people", is designated as the owner of the natural resource.'[50]

For the sustainability of any development process in society, the distribution of public goods has to be equitable and transparent. 'As natural resources are public goods, the doctrine of equality, which emerges from the concepts of justice and fairness, must guide the State in determining the actual mechanism for distribution of natural resources. In this regard, the doctrine of equality has two aspects: first, it regulates the rights and obligations of the State vis-à-vis its people and demands that the people be granted equitable access to natural resources and/or its products and that they are adequately compensated for the transfer of the resource to the private domain; and second, it regulates the rights and obligations of the State vis-à-vis private parties seeking to acquire/use the resource and demands that the procedure adopted for distribution is just, non-arbitrary and transparent and that it does not discriminate between similarly placed private parties.'[51]

---

[50] Ibid.

[51] Ibid.

In *Nagesh and Anr. v. Union of India (UOI) and Others*,[52] the High Court of Madhya Pradesh has ruled that 'in its initial stage the directive principles were approached, considered and treated in a pure legalistic approach but there have been cases pointing to bold steps towards a social welfare concept of the State in an era of judicial activism giving new dimension to these directive principles. Article 39(b) of the Constitution provides for equitable distribution of material resources. And this word "distribution" used in Article 39(b) need to be liberally construed so as to give full and comprehensive effect to the mandate of equitable distribution as contained in Article 39(b) of the Constitution'.[53]

The state is the legal owner and trustee of its people, and it must ensure that the process of distribution is guided by the doctrine of equality and larger public good. Sustainable development can be secured only when it happens for all. The right to livelihood has been declared by the constitutional courts of India as part and parcel of the fundamental right to life guaranteed under article 21 of the Constitution of India. To ensure the fundamental right to livelihood is fundamental to state policy, and it must be ensured through the equitable distribution of resources.

Sustainable State and Governance

A sustainable state having a sustainable form of governance is the next stage of development in the idea of 'the state' moving ahead from 'the welfare state'. Most modern and contemporary states are not only concerned with the welfare of its people, but they also have taken up the task of ensuring the fair process of justice and good governance. 'For the first time, States in the west are faced with the task of reshaping the society in order to ensure its survival. For that to succeed, the State has to commit itself to certain values which it renders legitimate and obligatory for all, and on the basis of those values, it plans and implements substantive changes of society and its institutions. It is a fact that the State still prefers to be led or motivated by the market, but it does not shirk the responsibility for strategic planning. We have therefore come a long way from the liberal State which rejected governmental paternalism. Awareness of the danger that threatens

---

[52]   1993 JLJ 746.

[53]   Ibid.

the continuation of life on our planet is necessary and sufficient explanation of the great responsibility undertaken by the State to realize sustainable development.'[54]

Dominance over resources and distribution through government agencies was an unwanted phenomenon in the concept of the state when it was asked to *wither away* from economic activities. A whole century of the Industrial Revolution in Britain and other now-developed countries has resulted in haphazard growth patterns and severe strain on earth's environment and ecology as a whole.

Now the state is again looked upon for more and more participation in the equitable distribution of resources and protection and preservation of the environment and ecology largely because of the failure of nonstate entities to balance economic growth with the socioeconomic betterment of the people. It proves that we are moving ahead from a police state to a liberal state further towards a sustainable state. Figure 4 highlights the stages in the development of the state concept.

Figure 4. Stages in the Development of State Concept

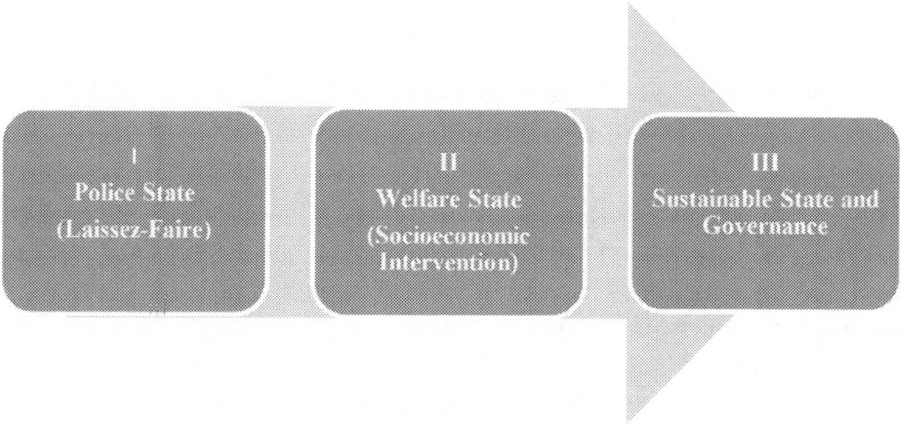

I Police State (Laissez-Faire)	II Welfare State (Socioeconomic Intervention)	III Sustainable State and Governance

---

54 Michael Decleris, *The Law of Sustainable Development: General Principles*, Office for Official Publications of the European Communities, European Commission, 2000, p. 41.

'In the past, society did not tolerate State dominance when it came to the distribution of wealth. Now, however, it cannot reject that dominance when its survival is at stake. Having accepted the leadership of the State in achieving the objective of survival, society must however accept a whole bundle of objectives whereby survival will be ensured. As we said in the brief analysis of Agenda 21, those objectives go far beyond mere economic policy and in fact aim to reform society so as to make it more just. So in our times survival is impossible without justice, and the justice of sustainable development is not merely the social policy exercised until now. Thus, the coercive state in the west is ceding its place to a state which will not only guarantee but bring about the ideal of Justice. The conclusion, then, is that for western States to succeed in that task they must amend the Roman tradition by returning to the classical Greek notion of just Polity, at whose disposal they will place the increased efficacy of the methods of scientific public policy. Power-games and persuasions are displaced to secondary status when not abandoned entirely. Justice, information, education and scientific management are the means of the new state policy.'[55]

New Delhi Principles of International Sustainable Development Law

The 70th Conference of the International Law Association (ILA), held in New Delhi, India, on 2–6 April 2002 for the purpose of identifying the substantive and procedural principles of international sustainable development law (hereinafter called ISDL), was concluded with 'New Delhi Declaration on the Principles of International Law related to Sustainable Development'.[56]

Seven *core principles* if ISDL were identified by the New Delhi Declaration (see table below). The New Delhi Declaration of the principles of ISDL was a conscious attempt to bring together sustainable development with the rhetoric and substance of human rights. Its preamble notes, 'The realization of the international bill of human rights, comprising economic,

---

[55]   Ibid.

[56]   See 'International Law Association New Delhi Declaration on Principles of International Law Relating to Sustainable Development' (London: ILA, 2002), report published by Kluwer Academic Publishers, available at http://cisdl.org/tribunals/pdf/NewDelhiDeclaration.pdf.

social and cultural rights, civil and political rights and peoples' rights, is central to the pursuance of sustainable development.'[57] Table 2 below provides the main ISDL principles developed.

Table 2. ISDL Principles

ISDL	Core Principles
Principle 1	The duty of states to ensure sustainable use of natural resources
Principle 2	The principle of equity and the eradication of poverty
Principle 3	The principle of common but differentiated responsibilities
Principle 4	The principle of the precautionary approach to human health, natural resources, and ecosystems
Principle 5	The principle of participation and access to information and justice
Principle 6	The principle of good governance
Principle 7	The principle of integration and interrelationship (in particular, in relation to human rights and social, economic, and environmental objectives)

In modern systems of nation states, every state has sovereignty over its natural resources. *Principle 1* enjoins upon all the states to use their natural resources in their territorial jurisdictions with rationality and a reasonable concern for all humankind. Conservation and care of fauna and flora as well as proper management of climate systems are a common concern for all humankind. Climate change and environmental hazards affect people across national boundaries. *Principle 2* calls for the equity and eradication of poverty. It is a self-explaining idea. In fact, equity in action is the first step to be adopted for the eradication of poverty. Indian jurisprudence on sustainable development was started by then prime minister of India Smt.

---

[57] International Law Association, Berlin Conference (2004), International Law On Sustainable Development, First Report, p. 5; report available at http://www.ila-hq. org/en/committees/index.cfm/cid/1017.

Indira Gandhi when, at the Stockholm Conference, she called poverty as the biggest polluter and hurdle in the way of sustainable development. Principles of equity include intergenerational equity as well as intragenerational equity. Intergenerational equity connotes the idea about the duty of the present generation for the future ones. It mandates on the present habitants of earth to use its resources in a way that it does not undermine the capacity of any future generation to use these resources. Intragenerational equity enjoins the people and states to utilise the resources in a way that can benefit all.

Gandhian philosophy of trusteeship explains the idea of intragenerational equity. Gandhian 'trusteeship provides a means of transforming the present capitalist order of society into an egalitarian one. It gives no quarter to capitalism, but gives the present owning class a chance of reforming itself. It is based on the faith that human nature is never beyond redemption. It does not recognize any right of private ownership of property except so far as it may be permitted by society for its own welfare. It does not exclude legislative regulation of the ownership and use of wealth. Thus under State-regulated trusteeship, an individual will not be free to hold or use his wealth for selfish satisfaction or in disregard of the interests of society. Just as it is proposed to fix a decent minimum living wage, even so a limit should be fixed for the maximum income that would be allowed to any person in society. The difference between such minimum and maximum incomes should be reasonable and equitable and variable from time to time so much so that the tendency would be towards obliteration of the difference. Under the Gandhian economic order the character of production will be determined by social necessity and not by personal whim or greed'.[58]

International sustainable development law may be called a soft law or merely a guiding principle for the states, but in an era where sovereignty rules international jurisprudence, the ISDL principles are the only hope to unite world consciousness. At the Delhi Sustainable Development Summit of 2013, held at New Delhi on 31 January to 2 February 2013, a new ISDL principle of *resource-efficient growth* was recognised and given emphasis under the aegis of the Energy Research Organization of New Delhi. It started with the theme 'The Global Challenge of Resource-Efficient Growth and Development'. No less than the prime minister of the country emphasised the

---

[58] Gandhian idea of trusteeship, a summary of the idea was published in *Harijan* in the issue dated 25 October 1952; text available at http://www.gandhimanibhavan.org.

need for sustainable utilisation of resources. While delivering the inaugural address, Dr. Manmohan Singh said, 'Humanity has traditionally put its faith in advances of technology to resolve problems of resource scarcities. However, there is now a growing realization that there may be no easy alternatives for some resources, particularly environmental resources. Resource efficiency is, thus, a necessary condition for sustainable development, and a key element of the economic pillar of sustainability. In addition, there are genuine concerns that in an unequal world, scarcity of resources would affect the poor more adversely, and key resources may become accessible only to a small section of people on this planet, leading to the exclusion of a large number of people who live in poverty and persistent deprivation. Resource efficiency is thus a critical element of inclusive growth and development agenda. The challenge is to build resilient and efficient economies, which will eradicate poverty and also ensure that the poor, already living on the margins of survival, are not made even more vulnerable. As a corollary, we should enhance efforts to develop technologies that ensure efficiency gains, which allow for more equitable distribution and use of these available resources. A global growth model, which is both inclusive and sustainable, would also assist developing countries to pursue their national development objectives.'[59]

---

[59] Prime Minister Dr. Manmohan Singh's address at the Delhi Sustainable Development Summit of 2013, New Delhi, on 31 January 2013.

CHAPTER III

INTERNATIONAL LAW ON SUSTAINABLE DEVELOPMENT

A contemporary evolutionary process of the principles of sustainable development law formally started with the Declaration of the United Nations Conference on the Human Environment in Stockholm in 1972. Here, the relationship of man and its environment was defined as 'man is both creature and moulder of his environment, which gives him physical sustenance and affords him the opportunity for intellectual, moral, social and spiritual growth'.[60]

Following the Stockholm Declaration, in 1987, a report by a group of legal experts on the principles of international law for the protection of the environment and sustainable development, which accompanied the report of the World Commission on Environment and Development (or the Brundtland Commission), entitled 'Our Common Future' was published. 'Our Common Future proposed the adoption of 22 legal principles, divided into four groups, meant to address the challenges identified in the report and to guide future law-making in the areas of environmental protection and sustainable development.'[61]

The United Nations Conference on Environment and Development (or Earth Summit) in 1992 produced a set of principles for sustainable development called the 1992 Rio Declaration and a plan for global sustainability called Agenda 21.[62] The figure below provides the evolutionary process of international sustainable development law.

---

[60] See Stockholm Declaration, the United Nations Conference on the Human Environment, Stockholm, 1972; available at http://www.unep.org/Documents, last visited on 6 May 2012.

[61] See the Report of the World Commission on Environment and Development: 'Our Common Future', 1987, United Nations; available at http://www.un-documents.net/our-common-future.pdf.

[62] See Rio Declaration on Environment and Development, United Nations Conference on Environment and Development, 1992, p. 1; available at http://www.unep.org/Documents.

Figure 1. Evolution of International Sustainable Development Law

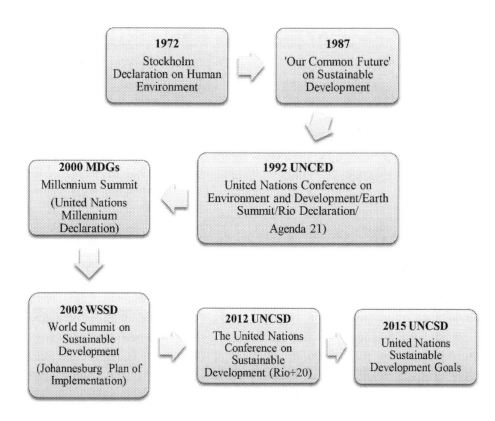

The Stockholm Declaration, the Report of the Brundtland Commission (also known as the World Commission on Environment and Development, WCED), and the Rio Declaration are three important international instruments that refer to sustainable development and its components. The Stockholm Declaration of 1972 made no specific reference to sustainable development, but its principles elucidate its components. The Brundtland Report provided the most widely recognised definitions of sustainable development: 'Sustainable development is development that meets the needs of the present without compromising the ability of future generations to meet their own needs.'[63] The Rio Declaration on Environment and Development (UNCED) of 1992—a successor of the Stockholm Declaration, which is

---

[63]   Supra note 60.

recognised as a landmark legal authority on the subject—addressed reversing the effects of environmental degradation 'in the context of increased national and international efforts to promote sustainable and environmentally sound development in all countries'.[64] Major international instruments are as follows:

1. Stockholm Declaration, 1972

1.1   The UN Conference on the Human Environment held in Stockholm marked the beginning of an international framework for sustainable development. It was the first major international gathering to discuss sustainable development at a global scale. In June 1972, representatives from 113 nations met in Stockholm at the United Nations Conference on the Human Environment. The Stockholm Conference was the first attempt by the international community to address the relationship between the environment and development at a global level. The conference was a success and put the environment on the global agenda. The Stockholm Action Plan, the first global action plan for the environment, provided the basis for a standard agenda and a common policy framework to deal with the first generation of environmental action. It was adopted in this conference. An important outcome of the conference was the establishment of the United Nations Environment Program (UNEP).[65]

1.2   At the Stockholm Conference, the late Mrs. Indira Gandhi, presenting the case of developing countries' basic needs, rightly pointed out, 'We don't wish to impoverish the environment any further and yet we cannot for a moment

---

[64]   Supra note 61.

[65]   See http://www.unep.org/.

forget the grim poverty of large number of people. Are not the poverty and need the greatest polluters?'[66]

1.3   The Stockholm Declaration was the pioneer in explicitly recognising the right to a healthy environment. It places importance on protecting both species and their habitat. The outcome of the conference was the statement on the Declaration on the Human Environment, a statement containing 26 principles and 109 recommendations, which are commonly referred to as the Stockholm Declaration. It was the Stockholm Declaration that has led to the development of international environmental law. Another outcome of the Stockholm Conference was Principle 21 of the declaration, which provided for the law of 'good neighborliness'. Principle 21 of the 1972 Stockholm Declaration states, 'States have, in accordance with the Charter of the United Nations and the principles of international law, the sovereign right to exploit their own resources pursuant to their own environmental policies, and the responsibility to ensure that activities within their jurisdiction or control do not cause damage to the environment of other States or of areas beyond the limits of national jurisdiction.'[67]

1.4   Principle 24 of the 1972 Stockholm Declaration talks about the duty to cooperate: 'International matters concerning the protection and improvement of the environment should be handled in a co-operative spirit by all countries, big and small, on an equal footing. Co-operation through multilateral or bilateral arrangements or other appropriate means is essential to effectively control, prevent, reduce and eliminate adverse environmental effects resulting from activities conducted in all spheres; in such a way that due account is taken of the

---

[66]   Smt. Indira Gandhi, 'Man and Environment', plenary session of the United Nations Conference on Human Environment, Stockholm, 1972, p. 2.

[67]   Supra note 60.

sovereignty and interests of all States.'[68] The table below shows the twenty-six principles of the Stockholm Declaration.

Table 1. 26 Principles of the Stockholm Declaration, 1972	
Principle 1	**Human rights are to be asserted; apartheid and colonialism are to be condemned.**
Principle 2	**Natural resources are to be safeguarded.**
Principle 3	**Earth's capacity to produce renewable resources are to be maintained.**
Principle 4	**Wildlife is to be safeguarded.**
Principle 5	**Nonrenewable resources are to be shared and not exhausted.**
Principle 6	**Pollution is not to exceed the environment's capacity to clean itself.**
Principle 7	**Damaging oceanic pollution is to be prevented.**
Principle 8	**Development is needed to improve the environment.**
Principle 9	**Developing countries, therefore, need assistance**
Principle 10	**Developing countries need reasonable prices for exports to carry out environmental management.**
Principle 11	**Environment policy needs to be established not to hamper development.**
Principle 12	**Developing countries need money to develop environmental safeguards.**
Principle 13	**Integrated development planning is needed.**
Principle 14	**Rational planning should resolve conflicts between the environment and development.**
Principle 15	**Human settlements must be planned to eliminate environmental problems.**
Principle 16	**Governments should plan their own appropriate population policies.**

---

[68]   Ibid.

Principle 17	National institutions must plan the development of states' natural resources.
Principle 18	Science and technology must be applied to the identification, avoidance, and control of environmental risks and the solution of environmental problems.
Principle 19	Environmental education is essential.
Principle 20	Environmental research must be promoted, particularly in developing countries.
Principle 21	States may use their resources as they wish but must not endanger others.
Principle 22	Compensation is due to states thus endangered.
Principle 23	Each nation must establish its own standards.
Principle 24	There must be cooperation on international issues.
Principle 25	International organisations should help to improve the environment.
Principle 26	Weapons of mass destruction must be eliminated.

2. Report of the World Commission on Environment and Development, 1987 ('Our Common Future')

2.1   The World Commission on Environment and Development (WCED), known by the name of its chair Gro Harlem Brundtland, was convened by the United Nations in 1983; and its report titled 'Our Common Future'[69] was published in 1987. The former secretary general of the United Nations, Javier Pérez de Cuéllar, appointed Gro Harlem Brundtland, the former prime minister of Norway, as the chairman of the commission in December 1983. The United Nations General

---

[69]   See Report of the World Commission on Environment and Development, United Nations, 1987; available at http://worldinbalance.net/pdf/ 1987-brundtland.pdf.

Assembly recognised the need to address the deterioration of the human environment and natural resources and to bring countries together to work to pursue sustainable development. This resulted in the establishment of the Brundtland Commission. The Brundtland Commission was officially dissolved in December 1987, subsequent to the release of the Brundtland Report in October 1987. The organisation Center for Our Common Future was established in place of the commission in April 1988. The Brundtland Commission formally recognised that environmental problems are global in nature and determined that it was in the common interest of all nations to establish policies for sustainable development.

2.2   The Report of the Brundtland Commission came up as 'Our Common Future',[70] and this report defined the concept of sustainable development as follows: 'Sustainable development is development that meets the needs of the present without compromising the ability of future generations to meet their own needs. It contains within it two key concepts: "the concept of needs, in particular the essential needs of the world's poor, to which overriding priority should be given"; and "the idea of limitations imposed by the state of technology and social organization on the environment's ability to meet present and future".'[71]

2.3   It has made suggestions in regard to the conflict between the environment and development. The commission suggested that development that is sustainable (i.e. which would meet the needs of the poor and address environmental issues) is acceptable. In the developing world, basic needs like adequate food, clean water, proper shelter, energy, etc., are still unanswered. Lack of development and poverty are the

---

[70]   Supra note 61.

[71]   Ibid.

biggest polluters. For example, in the state of Uttarakhand, developmental needs are in direct confrontation with environmental protection where many areas of the state are still without electricity supply. The state has been projected to be an energy state. The idea of sustainable development has emerged as an attempt to deal with environmental problems caused by economic growth. There are varied interpretations of the concept of sustainable development, but its primary purpose is to accomplish the process of economic development without causing destruction to the environment.

2.4   The Brundtland Report stated that critical 'global environmental problems were primarily the result of the enormous poverty of the South and the non-sustainable patterns of consumption and production in the North'.[72] The report evokes the spirit of the United Nations Conference on the Human Environment—the Stockholm Conference—which placed environmental concerns on the forefront of the political development sphere. Similarly, the Brundtland Report placed environmental issues firmly on the political agenda; it aimed to discuss the environment and development as the two sides of the same coin. The publication of 'Our Common Future' and the work of the World Commission on Environment and Development laid the groundwork for the convening of the Earth Summit in 1992 and the adoption of Agenda 21 as well as the establishment of the United Nations Commission on Sustainable Development, which aimed to monitor and report on the implementation of the Earth Summit agreements.

---

[72]   Ibid.

3. United Nations Conference on Environment and Development, 1992 (Earth Summit)

3.1   In June 1992, world leaders met in Rio de Janeiro at the United Nations Conference on Environment and Development (UNCED) for a summit largely known as Earth Summit. Marking the twentieth anniversary of the Stockholm Conference, members of the Earth Summit adopted the Rio Declaration on Environment and Development. The conference was a significant turning point to redirect national and international policies towards the integration of environmental dimensions into economic and developmental objectives. The Rio Declaration contained twenty-seven principles of sustainable development, including principle 7 on 'common but differentiated responsibilities', which states the following: 'In view of the different contributions to global environmental degradation, States have common but differentiated responsibilities. The developed countries acknowledge the responsibility that they bear in the international pursuit of sustainable development in view of the pressures their societies place on the global environment and of the technologies and financial resources they command.'[73]

3.2   The outcome of the conference—in particular, Agenda 21 and the Rio Principles—became instrumental in promoting the development and strengthening of institutional architecture for environmental protection and sustainable development at the national and international levels. The Rio Declaration contained twenty-seven principles of

---

[73]   See Rio Declaration on Environment and Development, the United Nations Conference on Environment and Development, having met at Rio de Janeiro from 3–14 June 1992; available at www.un.org.

sustainable development, including principle 7 on 'common but differentiated responsibilities' which states the following: 'States shall cooperate in a spirit of global partnership to conserve, protect and restore the health and integrity of the Earth's ecosystem. In view of the different contributions to global environmental degradation, States have common but differentiated responsibilities. The developed countries acknowledge the responsibility that they bear in the international pursuit to sustainable development in view of the pressures their societies place on the global environment and of the technologies and financial resources they command.' Following a recommendation in Agenda 21, the UN General Assembly officially created the Commission on Sustainable Development (CSD) later that year to review and monitor the implementation of Agenda 21.[74] The Earth Summit resulted in the following principles as shown in the table below:

Table 2. 27 Principles of the Rio Declaration	
Principle 1	Human beings are at the centre of concerns for sustainable development.
Principle 2	States have a sovereign right to exploit their own resources pursuant to their own environmental and developmental policies and not to cause damage to the environment of other states.
Principle 3	The right to development must be fulfilled so as to equitably meet the developmental and environmental needs of present and future generations.
Principle 4	To achieve sustainable development, environmental protection shall be an integral part of the development process and cannot be considered in isolation from it.

---

[74]   Ibid.

Principle 5	All states and all people shall cooperate in the essential task of eradicating poverty as an indispensable requirement for sustainable development in order to decrease the disparities in standards of living and better meet the needs of the majority of the people of the world.
Principle 6	The special situation and needs of developing countries, particularly the least developed and those most environmentally vulnerable, shall be given special priority. International actions in the field of environment and development should also address the interests and needs of all countries.
Principle 7	States shall cooperate in a spirit of global partnership to conserve, protect, and restore the health and integrity of the earth's ecosystem. In view of the different contributions to global environmental degradation, states have common but differentiated responsibilities. The developed countries acknowledge the responsibility that they bear in the international pursuit of sustainable development in view of the pressures their societies place on the global environment and of the technologies and financial resources they command.
Principle 8	To achieve sustainable development and a higher quality of life for all people, states should reduce and eliminate unsustainable patterns of production and consumption and promote appropriate demographic policies.
Principle 9	States should cooperate to strengthen endogenous capacity building for sustainable development by improving scientific understanding through exchanges of scientific and technological knowledge and by enhancing the development, adaptation, diffusion, and transfer of technologies, including new and innovative technologies.

Principle 10	Environmental issues are best handled with the participation of all concerned citizens at the relevant level. At the national level, each individual shall have appropriate access to information concerning the environment that is held by public authorities, including information on hazardous materials and activities in their communities, and the opportunity to participate in decision-making processes. States shall facilitate and encourage public awareness and participation by making information widely available. Effective access to judicial and administrative proceedings, including redress and remedy, shall be provided.
Principle 11	States shall enact effective environmental legislation. Environmental standards, management objectives, and priorities should reflect the environmental and developmental context to which they apply. Standards applied by some countries may be inappropriate and of unwarranted economic and social cost to other countries—in particular, developing countries.
Principle 12	States should cooperate to promote a supportive and open international economic system that would lead to economic growth and sustainable development in all countries and to better address the problems of environmental degradation. Trade policy measures for environmental purposes should not constitute a means of arbitrary or unjustifiable discrimination or a disguised restriction on international trade. Unilateral actions to deal with environmental challenges outside the jurisdiction of the importing country should be avoided. Environmental measures addressing transboundary or global environmental problems should, as far as possible, be based on an international consensus.

Principle 13	States shall develop national law regarding liability and compensation for the victims of pollution and other environmental damage. States shall also cooperate in an expeditious and more determined manner to develop further international law regarding liability and compensation for adverse effects of environmental damage caused by activities within their jurisdiction or control to areas beyond their jurisdiction.
Principle 14	States should effectively cooperate to discourage or prevent the relocation and transfer to other states any activities and substances that cause severe environmental degradation or are found to be harmful to human health.
Principle 15	In order to protect the environment, the precautionary approach shall be widely applied by states according to their capabilities. Where there are threats of serious or irreversible damage, lack of full scientific certainty shall not be used as a reason for postponing cost-effective measures to prevent environmental degradation.
Principle 16	National authorities should endeavour to promote the internalisation of environmental costs and the use of economic instruments, taking into account the approach that the polluter should, in principle, bear the cost of pollution, with due regard to the public interest and without distorting international trade and investment.
Principle 17	Environmental impact assessment, as a national instrument, shall be undertaken for proposed activities that are likely to have a significant adverse impact on the environment and are subject to a decision of a competent national authority.

Principle 18	States shall immediately notify other states of any natural disasters or other emergencies that are likely to produce sudden harmful effects on the environment of those states. Every effort shall be made by the international community to help states so afflicted.
Principle 19	States shall provide prior and timely notification and relevant information to potentially affected states on activities that may have a significant adverse transboundary environmental effect and shall consult with those states at an early stage and in good faith.
Principle 20	Women have a vital role in environmental management and development. Their full participation is therefore essential to achieve sustainable development.
Principle 21	The creativity, ideals, and courage of the youth of the world should be mobilised to forge a global partnership in order to achieve sustainable development and ensure a better future for all.
Principle 22	Indigenous people and their communities and other local communities have a vital role in environmental management and development because of their knowledge and traditional practices. States should recognise and duly support their identity, culture, and interests and enable their effective participation in the achievement of sustainable development.
Principle 23	The environment and natural resources of people under oppression, domination, and occupation shall be protected.
Principle 24	Warfare is inherently destructive of sustainable development. States shall therefore respect international law, providing protection for the environment in times of armed conflict and cooperating in its further development, as necessary.

Principle 25	Peace, development, and environmental protection are interdependent and indivisible.
Principle 26	States shall resolve all their environmental disputes peacefully and by appropriate means in accordance with the charter of the United Nations.
Principle 27	States and people shall cooperate in good faith and in a spirit of partnership in the fulfilment of the principles embodied in this declaration and in the further development of international law in the field of sustainable development.

4.   Agenda 21

4.1   This is a nonbinding and voluntarily implemented action plan of the United Nations in relation to sustainable development principles. It is also often referred to as Agenda 21. It was the output of the UN Conference on Environment and Development (UNCED). Agenda 21 refers to the twenty-first century, and its main principles are elucidated in the table below.

Table 3. Sections of Agenda 21		
Section I	Social and Economic Dimensions	**Combating poverty (especially in developing countries), changing consumption patterns, promoting health, achieving a more sustainable population, and sustainable settlement in decision making**
Section II	Conservation and Management of Resources for Development	**Atmospheric protection, combating deforestation, protecting fragile environments, conservation of biological diversity, control of pollution, and management of biotechnology and radioactive wastes**

Section III	Strengthening the Role of Major Groups	**Role of children and youth, women, NGOs, local authorities, businesses, and workers, as well as strengthening the roles of farmers and indigenous peoples and their communities**
Section IV	**Means of Implementation**	**Implementation to include science, technology transfer, education, international institutions, and financial mechanisms**

5.   Earth Summit + 5, 1997 in New York

5.1   In 1992, more than 100 heads of state met in Rio de Janeiro, Brazil, for the first international Earth Summit convened to address urgent problems of environmental protection and socioeconomic development. The assembled leaders signed the Convention on Climate Change and the Convention on Biological Diversity, endorsed the Rio Declaration and the Forest Principles, and adopted Agenda 21, a 300-page plan for achieving sustainable development in the twenty-first century.[75]

5.2   As a result of this landmark summit, the Commission on Sustainable Development (CSD) was created to monitor and report on the implementation of the Earth Summit agreements. This special session of the UN General Assembly took stock of how well countries, international organisations, and sectors of civil society have responded to the challenge of the Earth Summit. This was a special session of the General Assembly to review and appraise the

---

[75]   See the official website of the United Nations Earth Summit +5 available at https://www.un.org/esa/earthsummit/.

implementation of Agenda 21. The focus of this summit at this special session was to accelerate the implementation of Agenda 21 in a comprehensive manner and not to renegotiate its provisions or to be selective in its implementation. Further, it was affirmed by the participating parties that Agenda 21 remains the fundamental programme of action for achieving sustainable development and all the principles contained in the Rio Declaration on Environment and Development and the Forest Principles. All the nation heads reiterated their conviction that the achievement of sustainable development requires the integration of its economic, environmental, and social components and also recommitted to working together in the spirit of global partnership to reinforce our joint efforts to meet equitably the needs of present and future generations.

6. UN Millennium Development Goals (MDGs), 2000

6.1   At the outset of the new millennium, the Millennium Summit in September 2000 was called under the aegis of United Nations, which resulted into the largest gathering of world leaders in history. This also resulted into the adoption of the UN Millennium Declaration, which is committed to a new global partnership to reduce poverty and setting out a series of time-bound targets, with a deadline of the year 2015. These targets are generally known as Millennium Development Goals (MDGs). Through MDGs, for the first time, the world provided for itself time-bound and quantified targets to addressing extreme poverty in its many dimensions (e.g. income poverty, hunger, disease, lack of adequate shelter) and committed itself to the promotion of gender equality, education, and environmental sustainability. MDGs were recognised as basic human rights as the rights of each person on the planet to health, education, shelter, and security.

Eradicating poverty, achieving universal primary education, empowering women and promoting gender equality, reducing child mortality, improving maternal health, combating diseases like HIV, ensuring environmental sustainability, and developing a global partnership were identified as the major goals. All these goals are to be achieved necessarily for sustainable development. The figure below shows the MDGs categorically.

UN Millennium Development Goals

Goal 1
- Eradicate extreme hunger and poverty

Goal 2
- Achieve universal primary education

Goal 3
- Promote gender equality and empower women

Goal 4
- Reduce Child Mortality

Goal 5
- Improve Maternal Health

Goal 6
- Combat HIV/AIDS, Malaria and other diseases

Goal 7
- Ensure Environmental Sustainability

Goal 8
- Develop a Global Partnership for Development

7.   World Summit on Sustainable Development, 2002

7.1   The Earth Summit of 2002 is also referred as Rio+10 as it was held ten years after the Earth Summit in Rio de Janeiro. It was held in Johannesburg, South Africa, in September 2002. The Johannesburg Declaration and the Plan of Implementation of the World Summit on Sustainable Development were the main outputs of the summit. It is a successor to the United Nations Conference on the Human Environment at Stockholm in 1972 and the Earth Summit in Rio de Janeiro in 1992. While being a move towards committing states to uphold sustainable development, it looked at multilateralism as the way ahead.

The Johannesburg Plan of Implementation,[76] which was agreed to at the World Summit on Sustainable Development in 2002, recognised and reaffirmed these principles. It said, 'We strongly reaffirm our commitment to the Rio Principles,[77] the full implementation of Agenda 21[78] and the Program for the Further Implementation of Agenda 21. We also commit ourselves to achieving the internationally agreed development goals, including those contained in the United Nations Millennium Declaration and in the outcomes of the major United Nations conferences and international agreements since 1992.'[79]

The Johannesburg Plan of Implementation identified following workable areas of sustainable development: (a) poverty eradication, (b) changing unsustainable patterns of consumption and production, (c) protecting and managing the natural resource base of economic and social development, (d) sustainable development in a globalising world, (e) sustainable development of small island developing states, (f) sustainable development for Africa and others. It further identified the means of implementation for sustainable

---

[76]   See Johannesburg Summit, United Nations, 2002; report available at http://www. un.org/jsummit/html/basic_info/basicinfo.html.

[77]   Supra note 62.

[78]   Supra note 62.

[79]   Supra note 60.

development and began with 'the principle of common but differentiated responsibilities', which states the following: 'States shall cooperate in a spirit of global partnership to conserve, protect and restore the health and integrity of the Earth's ecosystem. In view of the different contributions to global environmental degradation, States have common but differentiated responsibilities. The developed countries acknowledge the responsibility that they bear in the international pursuit of sustainable development in view of the pressures their societies place on the global environment and of the technologies and financial resources they command.'[80]

The Johannesburg Plan of Implementation, as agreed to at the World Summit on Sustainable Development in 2002 (WSSD 2002), made a tectonic shift in the plan of sustainable development. It moved the world sustainable development jurisprudence from mere a environmental concern towards social and economic development. It resulted into the integration of the MDGs with sustainable development principles and practices. A workable implementation action plan and ideas are shown in the figure below. It shows that the action plan is executable and not mere a theoretical exercise. The figure below contains the most important of the action plans made in the Johannesburg Plan of Implementation.

---

[80] Supra note 60.

Figure 2. Workable Sustainable Development Principles

The Johannesburg Plan of Implementation

- Promote, facilitate, and finance, as appropriate, access to and the development, transfer, and diffusion of environmentally sound technologies and corresponding know-how, in particular to developing countries

- Encourage foreign direct investment in developing countries

- Resolve to take concerted action against international terrorism, which causes serious obstacles to sustainable development

- Encourage the private sector (including transnational corporations, private foundations, and civil society institutions) to provide financial and technical assistance to developing countries

- Estblish a global environment facility, which will enable it to address the funding requirements of new focal areas and existing ones and continue to be responsive to the needs and concerns of its recipient countries, in particular developing countries

- Implement speedily, effectively, and fully the enhanced heavily indebted poor countries (HIPC) initiatives

- Develop and promote the wider application of environmental impact assessments

- Call upon members of the World Trade Organization to fulfil the commitments made in the Doha Ministerial Declaration, notably in terms of market access, in particular for products of export interest to developing countries

- States should cooperate to promote a supportive and open international economic system that would lead to economic growth and sustainable development in all countries to better address the problems of environmental degradation

8.   New Delhi Declaration, 2002

8.1   The Rio Declaration is widely accepted as soft law, not
legally binding but nonetheless relevant to the development
of hard international law for sustainable development. The
Rio Declaration principles are reaffirmed and specifically
mentioned throughout Agenda 21. The Rio Declaration
was followed by the 'Report of the Expert Group Meeting
on Identification of Principles of International Law for
Sustainable Development', which was commissioned by the
UN Division for Sustainable Development in accordance
with a request by states at the second session of the UN
Commission on Sustainable Development in 1994. This
report, which was released in September 1995, identifies
nineteen principles and concepts of international law for
sustainable development based on the Rio Declaration,
Agenda 21, international treaties, and other legal instruments.

8.2   Following up on the recommendations of the report, the
Committee on the Legal Aspects of Sustainable Development
of the International Legal Association's released its New
Delhi ILA Declaration[81] on Principles of International Law
Relating to Sustainable Development as a resolution of the
70th Conference of the International Law Association in New
Delhi, India, on 2–6 April 2002. (The ILA has consultative
status as an international nongovernmental organisation
with a number of the United Nations specialised agencies.[82])
The declaration noted that sustainable development is now
widely accepted as a global objective and that the concept has
been amply recognised in various international and national

---

[81]   International Law Association, 'Report of the Seventieth Conference', New Delhi,
2002; available at http://www.ila-hq.org/en/publications/order-reports.cfm.

[82]   http://www.ila-hq.org/index.cfm.

legal instruments, including treaty law and jurisprudence at international and national levels.[83] It outlines seven principles of international law on sustainable development.

Table 4. Seven Principles of the International Law Association	
Principle 1	The duty of states to ensure sustainable use of natural resources
Principle 2	The principle of equity and the eradication of poverty
Principle 3	The principle of a precautionary approach to human health, natural resources, and ecosystems
Principle 4	The principle of public participation and access to information and justice
Principle 5	The principle of good governance
Principle 6	The principle of common but differentiated obligations
Principle 7	The principle of integration and interrelationship (in particular, in relation to human rights and social, economic, and environmental objectives)

The above-mentioned norms are not yet recognised as binding rules of customary international law. However, they are increasingly made operational in binding international treaties, forming part of international law and policy in the field of sustainable development, providing normative context for best policies and laws in the field, as well as in local Agenda 21 initiatives and national sustainable development strategies. Nico Schrijver, chair of the ILA Committee on International Law on Sustainable Development, presented the principles of the New Delhi Declaration as a 'first blueprint for the emerging field of sustainable development law and policy'.[84]

---

[83] Ibid.
[84] Supra note 4.

9.   The United Nations Conference on Sustainable Development, 2012 (Rio+20)

9.1   The United Nations Conference on Sustainable Development (UNCSD)[85] was organised in pursuance of a General Assembly resolution, and it took place in Brazil on 20–22 June 2012 to mark the twentieth anniversary of the 1992 United Nations Conference on Environment and Development (UNCED) in Rio de Janeiro and the tenth anniversary of the 2002 World Summit on Sustainable Development (WSSD) in Johannesburg; for these reasons, this conference is also known as Rio+20. Sharing our common vision, heads of states and governments and all other high-level representatives renewed their commitment to sustainable development and further resolved to ensure the promotion of an economically, socially, and environmentally sustainable future for our planet and for present and future generations. It also recognised poverty as the greatest global challenge to the world today and the eradication of poverty as an indispensable requirement for sustainable development. It also acknowledged the need to further mainstream sustainable development at all levels, integrating economic, social, and environmental aspects. It recalled the Stockholm Declaration of the United Nations Conference on the Human Environment, adopted at Stockholm on 16 June 1972, and reaffirmed all the principles of the Rio Declaration on Environment and Development, including, inter alia, the principle of common but differentiated responsibilities as set out in principle 7 of the Rio Declaration. Delegates reaffirmed the commitment to fully implement the Rio

---

[85]   See the Report of the United Nations Conference on Sustainable Development, Rio de Janeiro, Brazil, 2012; available at http://www.unep.org/Documents.

Declaration on Environment and Development, Agenda 21, the Program for the Further Implementation of Agenda 21, the Plan of Implementation of the World Summit on Sustainable Development (Johannesburg Plan of Implementation).

10.   The United Nations Sustainable Development Goals, 2015

10.1   On 25 September 2015, the United Nations prepared the 2030 Agenda for Sustainable Development and seventeen new sustainable development goals (SDGs). At the advent of 2016 on 1 January, seventeen SDGs of the 2030 Agenda for Sustainable Development came into force officially. These new bold and transformative SDGs are aimed at mobilising innovative efforts to end all forms of poverty, fight inequalities, and tackle climate change while ensuring that no one is left behind. To give an idea of the SDGs, the preamble of the declaration of the United Nations on SDGs is quoted below :

Preamble

This Agenda is a plan of action for people, planet and prosperity. It also seeks to strengthen universal peace in larger freedom. We recognize that eradicating poverty in all its forms and dimensions, including extreme poverty, is the greatest global challenge and an indispensable requirement for sustainable development. All countries and all stakeholders, acting in collaborative partnership, will implement this plan. We are resolved to free the human race from the tyranny of poverty and want and to heal and secure our planet. We are determined to take the bold and transformative steps which are urgently needed to shift the world onto a sustainable and resilient path. As we embark on this collective journey, we pledge that no one will be left behind. The 17 Sustainable Development Goals and 169 targets which we are announcing today demonstrate the scale and ambition of this new universal Agenda. They seek to build on the Millennium Development Goals and complete what these did not achieve. They seek to realize the human rights of all and to achieve gender equality and the empowerment of all women and girls. They are integrated and indivisible and balance the three dimensions of sustainable development: the economic, social and environmental. The Goals and targets will stimulate action over the next fifteen years in areas of critical importance for humanity and the planet.[86]

The succession of SDGs from MDGs are good for coherent and structured jurisprudence in this area through the institutionalisation of ideas of sustainable development because the institutionalisation of ideas with proper resource channelisation is needed for any stratified development of knowledge on sustainable development. The present UN agenda on sustainable development proves that anthropogenic sustainability challenges can be tackled by a transanthropocentric approach of development.

United Nations: Stepping Up for Development

UN Sustainable Development Goals

Goal 1.	End poverty in all its forms everywhere.
Goal 2.	End hunger, achieve food security and improved nutrition, and promote sustainable agriculture.

---

[86] Text of the declaration at http://www.un.org/pga/wp-content/uploads/sites/3/2015/08/120815_outcome-document-of-Summit-for-adoption-of-the-post-2015-development-agenda.pdf.

Goal 3.	Ensure healthy lives and promote well-being for all at all ages.
Goal 4.	Ensure inclusive and equitable-quality education and promote lifelong learning opportunities for all.
Goal 5.	Achieve gender equality and empower all women and girls.
Goal 6.	Ensure availability and sustainable management of water and sanitation for all.
Goal 7.	Ensure access to affordable, reliable, sustainable, and modern energy for all.
Goal 8.	Promote sustained, inclusive, and sustainable economic growth, full and productive employment, and decent work for all.
Goal 9.	Build resilient infrastructure, promote inclusive and sustainable industrialisation, and foster innovation.
Goal 10.	Reduce inequality within and among countries.
Goal 11.	Make cities and human settlements inclusive, safe, resilient, and sustainable.
Goal 12.	Ensure sustainable consumption and production patterns.
Goal 13.	Take urgent action to combat climate change and its impacts (acknowledging that the United Nations Framework Convention on Climate Change is the primary international and intergovernmental forum for negotiating the global response to climate change).
Goal 14	Conserve and sustainably use the oceans, seas, and marine resources for sustainable development.
Goal 15	Protect, restore, and promote sustainable use of terrestrial ecosystems, sustainably manage forests, combat desertification, stop and reverse land degradation, and halt biodiversity loss.
Goal 16	Promote peaceful and inclusive societies for sustainable development, provide access to justice for all, and build effective, accountable, and inclusive institutions at all levels.

Goal 17	Strengthen the means of implementation and revitalise global partnership for sustainable development.

SDGs are again in the arena of soft law and are not legally binding. They have been adopted by the United Nations and were left to the governments to own and establish national legal and policy frameworks to achieve seventeen goals. As was the case with the MDGs, the UN also relies on national governments to implement the SDGs through domestic sustainable development policies, plans, and programmes.

Implementation through national policy frameworks looks doubtful and as faulty as the predecessor scheme was (for MDGs). To countries like India and China who are rapidly industrialising their economies and primarily concentrating on economic growth, any sustainability concern may not seem primary. SDGs can only be achieved when equity in 'world resource distribution' and a 'fair balance in global economy' is reached, the onus of which lies with the countries already developed who have a 'sustainability debt' to repay to the world.

CHAPTER IV

SUSTAINABLE DEVELOPMENT IN INDIAN LEGAL FRAMEWORK

Ancient Indian Jurisprudence on Sustainable Development

Ancient Indian jurisprudence is well balanced with principles of sustainable development. The whole idea of living was based on harmonious coexistence with nature. 'Ma hinsyah sarva bhutani is a lesson of the Rig Veda, meaning, "Do not harm anything".'[87] Elements of nature were respected to the extent that they were personified as gods and worshipped. 'Nearly all the higher gods of the Rig Veda are personifications of natural phenomena, such as the sun, dawn, fire, wind and rain.'[88] Religion was the guiding force of the behaviour of people in almost every area of life in ancient India. State policies were also guided by religious principles. Hindus, the people who lived in ancient India, largely followed the Hindu religion. It is also known as Sanatana Dharma, which means 'religion,' which is sustained in perpetuity. Two of its core beliefs are that of tolerance and pluralism. These concepts are the very essence of Hinduism and are expressed through the diversity of Hindu practices and centuries of peaceful existence.

By accepting the divinity in all beings, living and nonliving, Hinduism views the universe as a family or, in Sanskrit, *Vasudhaiva Kutumbakam*. All beings, from the smallest organism to man, are considered manifestations of God. Mankind carries a special responsibility, as it is believed to be the most spiritually evolved with the capacity to not only tolerate, but honour the underlying equality and unity of all beings. 'Today, most discussions on environmentalism in our country begin with the Stockholm Conference (1972). But, some ancient texts tell us that our society paid more attention to

---

[87]   Akshoy K. Majumdar, *The Hindu History*, Rupa and Co., New Delhi. 2010, p. 182.
[88]   Id. at p. 188.

protecting the environment than we can imagine. These texts tell us that it was the dharma of each individual in society to protect Nature, so much so that people worshipped the objects of Nature. Trees, water, land and animals had considerable importance in our ancient texts; and the Manusmriti prescribed different punishments for causing injury to plants.'[89] It is clear from the above reference that environmental protection and pollution control were made duties for the whole society instead of the responsibility of an individual or a village. Duty was cast on the society as a whole to protect and preserve the environment, leading to sustainable development.

Ancient Indian religion was based on the well-being of all. 'May all beings be happy', 'may all beings be healthy', 'may all beings experience prosperity', 'may none in the world suffer' were the predominant ideas of ancient Indian philosophy. These demonstrate how deeply the principles of sustainable development as to the social, economic, and environmental development of all were entrenched in the ideas of that period. Another hymn demonstrating the idea of sustainable universal well-being states the following: 'May peace radiate there in the whole sky as well as in the vast ethereal space everywhere. May peace reign all over this earth, in water and in all herbs, trees and creepers. May peace flow over the whole universe. May peace be in the Supreme Being Brahman. And may there always exist in all peace and peace alone. Om peace, peace and peace to us and all beings.'[90] Universality in the hymns of ancient Indian religious principles indicates the world view of the people of the time. It concerns nature as well as its inhabitants equally. It is the perfect balance of social, economic, and environmental concerns for all. The Atharvaveda proclaimed,

---

[89] Justice Madan B. Lokur, 'Environmental Law: Its Development and Jurisprudence', Lecture available at http://awsassets.wwfindia.org.

[90] Yajurveda 36:17

Sanskrit- ॐ द्यौः शान्तिरन्तरिक्षँ शान्तिः, पृथिवी शान्तिरापः शान्तिरोषधयः शान्तिः । वनस्पतयः शान्तिर्विश्वे देवाः शान्तिर्ब्रह्म शान्तिः, सर्वँ शान्तिः शान्तिरेव शान्तिः सा मा शान्तिरेधि ॥, ॐ शान्तिः शान्तिः शान्तिः ॥

English-*Om Dyauḥ Śāntirantarikṣaṁ Śāntiḥ, Pṛthivī Śāntirāpaḥ Śāntiroṣadhayaḥ Śāntiḥ Vanaspatayaḥ Śāntirviśvedevāḥ Śāntirbrahma Śāntiḥ, Sarvaṁ Śāntiḥ Śāntireva Śāntiḥ Sā Mā Śāntiredhi, Om Śāntiḥ, Śāntiḥ, Śāntiḥ.*

'Man's paradise is on the earth. This living world is a beloved place for all. It has blessings of nature's bounties and love in lovely spirit.'[91] A high regard for traditions in India has ensured that sustainable development values are incorporated into the social and legal norms of modern society.

Sustainable Development in Kautilya's *Arthashastra*

Arthashastra is an ancient Indian book on politics and governance written by Chanakya (also named Kautilya), who was the prime minister of Chandragupta Maurya, the king of the Mauryan empire. The name of the book suggests that it is about economics, but it is only in contemporary context that *arthashastra* is meant as economics. In ancient India, the meaning of the word *arthashastra* means everything from economics to politics, and governance came under the same subject. Although it is basically about governance and the rights and duties of the kings and princes, it also serves as a guide on how various sections of society should be taken care of. The whole treatise of *Arthashastra* is in fourteen books that discuss a wide range of subjects, including administration, law, industry, commerce, and foreign policy. Book 2 deals with the subject of the environment. The duties of government superintendents have been defined in chapter 1, 'Formation of Villages'. The king has been ordained to set up new forests. It says, 'Thus the king shall not only keep in good repair timber and elephant forests, buildings, and mines created in the past, but also set up new ones.'

Wildlife, reserve forests, and separate pathways for animals were important areas of government concern in the Mauryan empire. State-employed animal doctors were in service. Chapter 26 provided various punishments for any person who kills an animal under state protection. Chapter 26 directed that 'when a person entraps, kills, or molests deer, bison, birds, and fish which are declared to be under State protection or which live in forests under State-protection (abhayáranya), he shall be punished. Householders trespassing in forest preserves shall be punished'.

The social, economic, and environmental components of the modern-day concept of sustainable development were adequately represented in ancient Indian life. Out of the three, we see in the *Arthashastra* the concern for forests, and wildlife finds repeated mention. Society was largely egalitarian,

---

[91]   *Supreme Court Journal*, Supreme Court of India, 1995, p. 74.

and the state took adequate care of the welfare of its people in the Mauryan empire. Repeated concern for forests and wildlife shows how the state took special care of them.

Principles of Sustainable Development in King Ashoka's Rock Edicts

Ashoka was the great emperor of India in the third century BCE. He was well known as the king of peace. He was born around 300 BCE. He had a life of seventy years, with nearly forty years as king. The Mauryan empire reached its pinnacle but started to decline after the long rule of King Ashoka. However, the principles of Dhamma became the tenets of official state policy during his rule. 'The policy of Dhamma included the state's concern for the welfare of its people. The Emperor claims that: On the roads I have had banyan trees planted, which will give the shade to beasts and men. I have had mango groves planted and I have had wells dug and rest houses built every nine miles . . . And I have had many watering places made everywhere for the use of beasts and men. But this benefit is important, and indeed the world has enjoyed attention in many ways from former kings as well as from me. But I have done these things in order that my people might conform to Dhamma (Pillar Edict VII, translated by Romila Thapar).'[92]

The principles of sustainable development in the form of social welfare and the economic well-being of subjects became the prime concerns of the state after King Ashoka adopted Buddhism as the state's religion. State protection was provisioned for forests, wildlife, and other natural habitats. The government passed instructions for the general public through various rock edicts. In the Fifth Pillar Edict of the Seven Pillar Edicts,' King Ashoka declares, 'Beloved-of-the-Gods, King Piyadasi, speaks thus: Twenty-six years after my coronation various animals were declared to be protected— parrots, mainas, aruna, ruddy geese, wild ducks, nandimukhas, gelatas, bats, queen ants, terrapins, boneless fish, vedareyaka, gangapuputaka, sankiya fish, tortoises, porcupines, squirrels, deer, bulls, okapinda, wild asses, wild pigeons, domestic pigeons and all four-footed creatures that are neither useful nor edible. Those nanny goats, ewes and sows which are with young or giving milk to their young are protected, and so are young ones less than

---

[92]   Romila Thapar, *Ashoka and the Decline of Mauryas*, Oxford University Press, New Delhi, 1998, p. 265.

six months old. Cocks are not to be caponized, husks hiding living beings are not to be burnt and forests are not to be burnt either without reason or to kill creatures.'[93]

Sustainable Development in the British Era

The development of what came to be known as Anglo-Indian law was a tortuous process involving many contradictions in principle and practice. Whereas the East India Company began in the seventeenth century in Bombay to build a system of jurisprudence that called for absolute respect for local custom and usage, by the nineteenth century, its government in Bengal had acquired sufficient confidence to attempt to influence some customs and usage through social legislation enforced by company courts.[94]

Colonial rules were established to exploit, not benefit, the colony. 'No exception to the rule' was the British rule in India. Prominent concern in all policy decisions was the exploitation of natural resources of the colony. Any concern for the environment or any care for economic growth could not be seen in the colonial period policies established by the English rulers in India. However, certain laws incidentally benefitted the colonial population. Under the influence and pressure of local leaders, the British brought into force various laws that helped the social development of the people of India. Regarding the principles of sustainable development, British rule in India was a disaster and was exploitative in nature. All the legislations were only in the form of another tool in the hands of the colonial masters to exploit India's natural resources. The unbridled exploitation of forests and their timber was one of the major causes of devastation of the environment in India at the hands of its colonial rulers. During the rule of the East India Company, there was absolutely no restriction in the cutting of trees in the forests and the killing of wildlife (in later part of the British rule, however, some reserve forests were marked, like Kaziranga and Corbett Park). After the transfer of power from the East India Company to the British government in 1857, the British government started securing the channels of constant supply of raw material, fuel, and timber for its factories in England by converting

---

[93] http://www.accesstoinsight.org/lib/authors/dhammika/wheel386.html.

[94] Nancy Gardner Cassels, ***Social Legislation of the East India Company***, Sage Publications India Pvt. Ltd., New Delhi, 2010, p. 3.

the forests into government property. The colonial mindset of the rulers are explicitly seen in the National Forest Policy of 1894, the first formal forest policy in India. This policy stipulated that 'forests which are the reservoirs of valuable timbers should be managed on commercial lines as a source of revenue to the States'.[95] Table 1 below shows the sustainability impact of British legislations on the Indian population.

British legislations were never intended for the benefit of the colonies, and certainly, India—despite being a crown jewel—was no exception to this rule. Most of the economic as well as environmental impacts were exploitative in nature; the only thing the Indian people benefitted from the colonial legislations were the social reforms.

The table below lists the impacts of major British legislations on the Indian population and also enumerates their sustainability factor.

---

[95]   Kulbhushan Balooni, 'Participatory Forest Management in India: An Analysis of Policy Trends amid Management Change', *Policy Trend Report*, Indian Institute of Management Kozhikode, 2002, pp. 88–113.

No.	British Legislation	Object		
		Environmental	**Social**	**Economic**
Table 1. Legislations in British India Influencing the Environmental, Social, and Economic Development of Natives				
1.	**The Shore Nuisance (Bombay and Kolaba) Act, 1853**	Earliest statute for control of water pollution in India. It was the first act in the field of environmental protection in India, enacted by the British Parliament for British India. This act was passed to ensure the safe navigation in the harbour of Bombay and generally for public interest to facilitate the removal of nuisances, obstructions, and encroachments.		
2.	**The Oriental Gas Company Act, 1857**	The Oriental Gas Company (OGC) Act was among the first acts in the field of water pollution. This act was passed with caution and regulation for the Orient Gas Company to do as little damage to the environment as may be in the execution of its supply projects and to compensate for any damage that may be done in the execution of such projects.		

3.	**Indian Penal Code, 1860**	Chapter 14 of the Indian Penal Code (IPC) from section 268 to 291 declares various forms of public nuisances. Any corruption of a body of water, air pollution, and noise pollution are also covered.		
4.	**The Sarais Act, 1867**	This act ordained the keeper of the Sarai to keep the drinking water free of all kinds of pollution and maintain a high level of hygiene in the Sarai. It was one of the duties of the Sarai keeper to inform the nearest police station about any person with any contagious or infectious disease.		
5.	**The North India Canal and Drainage Act, 1873**	Various punishments were provided for damaging bodies of water.		
6.	**The Obstruction in Fairways Act, 1881**	Section 8 of the act empowered the central government to make rules to regulate or prohibit the throwing of rubbish in any fairway leading to a port causing or likely to give rise to a bank or shoal.		

7.	**Indian Easements Act, 1882**	This protected riparian owners against unreasonable pollution by an upstream officer. Illustrations (f), (h), and (j) of section 7 of the act deal with pollution of waters. Section 28(d) of the 1882 Easement Act on the one hand allowed a prescriptive right to pollute the water, but it was not an absolute right. Illustrations (f), (g), and (j) of this section limited this prescriptive right not to unreasonably pollute or cause material injury to others.		
8.	**The Indian Fisheries Act, 1897**	This act contains seven sections. The killing of fish was declared illegal when poisoning water and when using explosives.		
9.	**Indian Ports Act, 1908**	The Indian Ports Act was passed for the regulation and prevention of water pollution caused by the use of oil or the discharging of oil in the port waters.		

10.	**Forest Acts of 1865 and 1878**	These acts were passed basically to declare the right of the state over all the forests and their right of exploitation. Colonial requirements of making a huge supply network of railways and the consequent need of timber were the prime objectives behind passing these acts.		
11.	**Forest Act of Madras, 1873**	This was for the protection of forests in the state of Madras.		
12.	**Elephant Preservation Act, 1879**	He killing and capture of wild elephants was prohibited. No person shall kill, injure, or capture or attempt to kill, injure, or capture any wild elephant, barring a few circumstances provided in the act.		
13.	**The Obstruction in Airways Act, 1881**	This was for the prevention of air pollution.		
14.	**Wild Birds Protection Act, 1887 (10 of 1887)**	This act enabled the then government to frame rules prohibiting the possession or sale of any kinds of specified wild birds, which have been killed or taken during the breeding season.		

15.	**Wild Birds and Animals Protection Act, 1912 (8 of 1912)**	This act of 1912 was amended in the year 1935 by the Wild Birds and Animals Protection (Amendment) Act, 1935 (27 of 1935).		
16.	**The Bengal Smoke Nuisance Act, 1905**	This was passed to prevent air pollution.		
17.	**The Explosives Act, 1908**	This was passed also to prevent air pollution.		
18.	**The Indian Forest Act, 1927**	This was passed with an objective to consolidate the law relating to forests, the transit of forest produce, and the duty leviable on timber and other forest produce. The act of 1927 also embodied a land-using policy whereby the British could acquire all forestland, village forests, and other common property resources. Section 26(i) of the act makes it punishable if any person who, in contravention of the rules made by the state government, poisons the water in a forested area. This act is still in force, together with several amendments made by the state governments.		

19.	Hailey National Park Act, 1936	This was passed to declare an area a reserve forest and for the protection of wildlife (now called Corbett National Park).		
20.	The Bihar Wastelands (Reclamation, Cultivation, and Improvement) Act, 1946	This was passed to bring the wastelands into cultivation.		There was an **improvement in the economic condition of the land tillers**
21.	Bengal Regulation XXI, 1795		Sections 9 and 11 prevented Brahmins in the province of Benares from wounding or killing their female relations or children. The law banned the practice of female infanticide and ended the exemption of Benares Brahmins from capital punishment.	The **female population increased, and as a result, the sex ratio of society became more balanced.**
22.	Bengal Regulation VIII, 1799		This discontinued the exemption in Muslim law from punishment of death for the wilful murder of a slave by his master.	

23.	**Bengal Regulation VI, 1802**		This prevented the sacrifice of children to the sharks at Saugor and other places.	
24.	**Bengal Regulation LIII, 1803**		This was the first company law to deal with dacoity as a crime.	
25.	**Bengal Regulation XI, 1806**		This banned slavery in Bengal. Section 8 ordained 'proper compensation for bearers, coolies, boatmen, carts or bullocks . . . and a just price for provisions'.	
26.	**Charter Act of 1813**		Major social reform was planned through this act of the British Parliament. Education of East India Company's Hindu and Muslim subjects was declared as the responsibility of the state.	

27.	**Bengal Regulation XVII, 1829**		This was passed on 4 December 1829. The law declared that inasmuch as 'the practice of suttee' was revolting to the feelings of human nature and was 'nowhere enjoined by the religion of the Hindoos as an imperative duty', it was 'hereby declared illegal'. Sati prevention law was the greatest development of the Indian legislative jurisprudence. It amounted to the boost in social development of the women in Bengal.	**Women became more independent, and their participation in society also increased.**
28.	**Madras Regulation I, 1830**		Governor Mountstuart Elphinstone followed the suit and abolished the practice of widow burning (sati) in Medras in the following year.	**Women became more independent, and their participation in society also increased**
29.	**Act XI of 1835**		Governor General Charles Metcalfe decided to enact the law by which the press was made free from all kinds of unnecessary censorship.	

30.	Thuggee and Dacoity Suppression Acts, 1836–1848		This was a series of acts that outlawed thuggee—a practice in North and Central India involving robbery and brutal murder and mutilation on highways.	**Highways became more safe and secure. Trade routes flourished.**
31.	Act V of 1843		By act 5 of 1843, the East India Company declared slavery to be illegal within its Indian territories.	**Slavery abolition improved the conditions of the labourers.**
32.	Caste Disabilities Removal Act, 1850		Caste system in Hindu families was reduced.	
33.	Act XV of 1856		This important act paved the way for the remarriage of Hindu widows hitherto prohibited as per the then customary Indian law.	
34.	Indian Penal Code, 1860		This streamlined definitions of various crimes and provided the punishments for them.	

Sustainable Development Jurisprudence in Independent India

The Constitution of India is the *Grundnorm* of sustainable development. One of the most prominent features of the Indian constitution is that it talks about the composite development of the people. We haven't seen much discussion on the environmental aspect in the constituent assembly debates, but the social and economic aspects of development are discussed in detail, and corresponding provisions were incorporated into the constitution. It has mandatory as well as directory provisions. It can be a guiding force for the whole world. At the very outset its 'preamble secures to all its people; JUSTICE, social, economic and political; LIBERTY of thought, expression, belief, faith and worship; EQUALITY of status and of opportunity'. Social and economic development are expressly secured in the legal framework of India. The protection and improvement of the natural environment saw the express provision in the Constitution of India for the first time in the form of the fundamental duty of a citizen enshrined in article 51A of the constitution.[96]

The environmental aspect has been read and interpreted by the Indian courts as a natural corollary to various other provisions of the constitution. Soon after the introduction of this vital fundamental duty of the citizen, the Indian Supreme Court recognised it as a very important landmark in the development of Indian sustainable development jurisprudence. While deciding the case of *Rural Litigation and Entitlement Kendra and Others v. State of Uttar Pradesh and Others*,[97] the court held the following: 'Consciousness for environmental protection is of recent origin. The United Nations Conference on World Environment held in Stockholm in June 1972 and the follow-up action thereafter is spreading the awareness. Over thousands of years men had been successfully exploiting the ecological system for his sustenance but with the growth of population the demand for land has increased and forest growth has been and is being cut down and man has started encroaching upon Nature and its assets. Scientific developments have made it possible and convenient for man to approach the places which were hitherto beyond his ken. The consequences of such

---

[96]   Section 11, Constitution (Forty-Second Amendment) Act, 1976, (w.e.f. 3 January 1977).

[97]   AIR 1987 SC 359.

interference with ecology and environment have now came to be realized. It is necessary that the Himalayas and the forest growth on the mountain range should be left un-interfered with so that there may be sufficient quantity of rain. The top soil may be preserved without being eroded and the natural setting of the area may remain intact. We had commended earlier to the State of Uttar Pradesh as also to the Union of India that afforestation activity may be carried out in the whole valley and the hills. We have been told that such activity has been undertaken. We are not oblivious of the fact that natural resources have got to be tapped for the purposes of social development but one cannot forget at the same time that tapping of resources have to be done with requisite attention and care so that ecology and environment may not be affected in any serious' way; there may not be any depletion of water resources and long-term planning must be undertaken to keep up the national wealth. It has always to be remembered that these are permanent assets of mankind and are not intended to be exhausted in one generation. We must place on record our appreciation of the steps taken by the Rural Litigation and Entitlement Kendra. But for this move, all that has happened perhaps may not have come. Preservation of the environment and keeping the ecological balance unaffected is a task which not only Governments but also every citizen must undertake. It is a social obligation and let us remind every Indian citizen that it is his fundamental duty as enshrined in Article 51 A (g) of the Constitution.'[98]

The right to a clean environment has been read and interpreted as part and parcel of the right to life enshrined under article 21 of the Constitution of India. Development—whether social, economic, or environmental—flows from various articles of the Constitution of India. The table below shows the facets of sustainable development principles enshrined in the Constitution of India. Each and every article in the table below guarantees and promotes sustainable development in a unique way.

---

[98] *Rural Litigation and Entitlement Kendra and Others v. State of Uttar Pradesh and Others*, AIR 1987 SC 359.

Sl.	Constitutional Provision	Development Objective		
		Environmental	Social	Economic
	Preamble		Justice, declared India to be a socialist state, mandating the welfare of the people as the primary concern of the state	**Justice, equality of opportunity**
	Article 14		Equality before law and the equal protection of laws	
	Article 15		Prohibition of discrimination on grounds of religion, race, caste, sex, or place of birth	
	Article 16			**Equality of opportunity in matters of public employment**
	Article 17		Abolition of untouchability	
	Article 18		Abolition of titles	
	Article 19		Protection of certain rights regarding freedom of speech and others: (1) All citizens shall have the right— (*a*) to freedom of speech and expression, (*b*) to assemble peaceably and without arms, (*c*) to form associations or unions, (*d*) to move freely throughout the territory of India, (*e*) to reside and settle in any part of the territory of India, and	**(*g*) to practise any profession or to carry on any occupation, trade, or business.**

Table 2. Facets of Sustainable Development Principles Enshrined in the Constitution of India

	Article 21	The right to a clean and healthy environment has been interpreted as part and parcel of the right to life by the Indian courts though various judicial pronouncements	Protection of life and personal liberty	
	Article 21A		Right to education	
	Article 23			**Prohibition of traffic in human beings and forced labour**
	Article 24		Prohibition of employment of children in factories and others	
	Article 29		Protection of interests of minorities	
	Article 32	**Remedies for enforcement of rights conferred by part 3 of the constitution.** **After the Hon'ble Supreme Court relaxed the rule of *locas standi* and gave birth to a new culture of public interest litigations, majority of the cases on the environment and for its protection have been filed and heard because of this hallmark article of the Constitution of India.**		
	Article 38		State to secure a social order for the promotion of the welfare of the people	

Article 39		Citizens, men and women equally, have the right to an adequate means of livelihood. Health and strength of workers, men and women, and the tender age of children are not abused and that citizens are not forced by economic necessity to enter vocations unsuited to their age or strength. Children are given opportunities and facilities to develop in a healthy manner and in conditions of freedom and dignity and that children and youth are protected against exploitation and against moral and material abandonment	**Ownership and control of material resources of the community are so distributed as best to subserve the common good.** **Operation of the economic system does not result in the concentration of wealth and means of production to the common detriment.** **There is equal pay for equal work for both men and women.**
Article 40		Organisation of village panchayats.	
Article 41			**Right to work**
Article 42			**Living wage and others for workers**
Article 47	Duty of the state to raise the level of nutrition and the standard of living and to improve public health		

	Article 48	Organisation of agriculture and animal husbandry	
	Article 48A	Protection and improvement of the environment and the safeguarding of forests and wildlife	
	Article 51A (g)	Fundamental duty of every citizen to protect and improve the natural environment, including forests, lakes, rivers, and wildlife, and to have compassion for living creatures	
	Article 226	**At the state level, every citizen has the right to approach the high court for the protection of the rights provided in the Constitution of India against the state. After the relaxation of the rule of *locas standi*, most of the public interest petitions are filed before the high courts under the article 226. Environmental protection has been a major area of litigation in the Indian courts, and a number of effective results have been achieved.**	

Schedules			
Legislative authority to the centre and state are distributed as per the lists of subjects provided in the Seventh Schedule to the Constitution of India. From the sustainable development point of view, such distribution is very important. The framers of the constitution were aware that various social, economic, and environmental problems have their different dimensions and that they need to be addressed at different levels of administration. Environmental problems must be addressed at the national level, while various social and economic problems need to be addressed at a much micro level. Keeping in view this spirit, the framers provided the separate subjects to be legislated by separate bodies.			
SEVENTH SCHEDULE LIST I	Entry 56. Regulation and development of inter-State rivers and river valleys to the extent to which such regulation and development under the control of the Union is declared by Parliament by law to be expedient in the public interest. Entry 57. Fishing and fisheries beyond territorial waters.		

SEVENTH SCHEDULE LIST II	Entry 6. Public health and sanitation; hospitals and dispensaries. Entry 17. Water, that is to say, water supplies, irrigation and canals, drainage and embankments, water storage and water power subject to the provisions of entry 56 of List I.		
SEVENTH SCHEDULE LIST III	**Entry 17. Prevention of cruelty to animals. Entry 17A. Forests. Entry 17B. Protection of wild animals and birds. Entry 36. Factories**	**Entry 20A. Population control and family planning.**	**Entry 24. Welfare of labour including conditions of work**

Sustainable Development in Indian National Policy Framework

After independence, India adopted the method of development through planning, and various plans every five years were made and implemented. These plans are the source of policy formation and are the guiding principles for legislation at different stages of the federal structure of India. Environment sustainability became evident from Fourth Plan onwards in India.

(a) Fourth Five-Year Plan (1969–1974)

Problems relating to the environment became the concern of Indian planning in this plan for the first time. The Fourth Plan laid down the following policy for the guidance of Indian legislative bodies:

> Planning for harmonious development recognizes the unity of nature and man. Such planning is possible only on the basis of a comprehensive appraisal of environmental issues. There are instances in which timely, specialized advice on environmental aspects could have helped in project design and in averting subsequent adverse effect on the environment leading to loss of invested resources. It is necessary, therefore, to introduce the environmental aspect into our planning and development.

(b) Tiwari Committee (1980)

In 1980, the Tiwari Committee was appointed by the government of India for the review of various environmental legislations in the country and for recommendations for their better implementation. This committee recommended the introduction of environmental protection in the concurrent list of the Seventh Schedule to the Constitution of India. It recommended the creation of the new Department for Environment.[99]

(c) Sixth Five-Year Plan (1980–1985)

In the Sixth Five-Year Plan, environment concern attracted more budgetary allocation, and a new Department of Environment was set up by the union government. The Wildlife Institute was also set up in 1982–1983 for the building up of scientific knowledge on wildlife research. Activities in the areas of water and air pollution control saw promotion. Training and awareness about environmental information were enhanced.

---

[99] See 'Report of the Committee on Review of Legislative Measures and Administrative Measures for Ensuring Environmental Protection', Department of Science and Technology, Government of India, New Delhi, 1980.

(d) Seventh Five-Year Plan (1985–1990)

The National Development Board was set up in 1985. The National Forest Policy was formulated in 1988 with the aim of ensuring environmental sustainability and maintenance of ecological balance. The implementation of the National Wildlife Plan was initiated. Programmes on waste recycling and the prevention of coastal pollution were initiated. Environment-impact assessments for major river valleys and hydroelectric, mining, industrial, and thermal power projects were carried out through the Environmental Appraisal Committee.

(e) Eighth Five-Year Plan (1992–1997)

Controlling pollution became the major concern of the government at all levels. The idea of controlling pollution at the source emerged. Criteria for eco-labelling of consumer products were developed. Vehicular pollution started being checked. Small-scale industries were promoted to take measures for environmental protection.

Various incentives were announced and introduced by the government to adopt efficiency for enhancing and waste minimisation practices like the enhancement of cess rates on water consumption, duty concessions on the import of certain pollution-control equipment, and accelerated depreciation on pollution abatement equipment. Capacity studies on the Doon Valley, the National Capital Region, and other like areas to improve methodologies and techniques of environment-impact assessment were carried out. BSI and ZSI surveys were conducted. In 1991–1992, a scheme on biodiversity conservation was initiated. Environment-impact assessment (hereinafter referred to as EIA) was introduced and made mandatory for majority of large developmental activities. EIA was developed as an important tool for integrating environmental concerns in the development process and for improved decision making. In 1994, the Ministry of Environment and Forests (hereinafter called MoEF) issued the first EIA notification prescribing mandatory environmental clearance for various development-related projects. The process involved consideration of environmental consequences before starting projects and included procedures like EIA study, public hearing in certain cases, and consideration of outcomes by expert groups before the issuing of a final clearance by the MoEF. Programmes such as

Man and Biosphere Programme, the Environmental Research Programme, and a research on climate change were undertaken. The National River Conservation Plan was also approved in 1995.[100]

(f) Ninth Five-Year Plan (1997–2002)

The Ninth Plan included attempts to phase out lead in motor spirit for improvement in the quality of high-speed diesel. This plan specially focused on the integration of environmental concerns with decision making. There were many area-specific programmes, like the National River Conservation Programme, which started the National Lake Conservation Programme. Taj Trapezium schemes to protect the Himalayan ecosystem and biodiversity. A special programme for sustainable development of islands was initiated, and in 1998, the Islands Development Authority (IDA) was constituted. Many schemes for afforestation and wetland development were also carried out.

(g) National Health Policy, 2002

The main objective of the National Health Policy (NHP) of 2002 is to achieve an acceptable standard of good health amongst the general population of the country. The approach is to increase access to the decentralised public health system by establishing new infrastructure in deficient areas and by upgrading the infrastructure in existing institutions. Overriding importance has been given to ensuring a more equitable access to health services across the social and geographical expanse of the country. The contribution of the private sector in providing health services would be enhanced, particularly for the population group that can afford to pay for services. Primacy shall be laid on preventive and first-line curative initiatives at the primary health level. Emphasis will be laid on the rational use of drugs within the allopathic system. Increased access to tried and tested systems of traditional medicine will be ensured.[101]

---

[100] See Eighth Five-Year Plan (1992–1997), Planning Commission, Government of India, New Delhi; available at http://planningcommission.nic.in/.

[101] See National Health Policy, Government of India, New Delhi, 2002; available at http://www.nrhmassam.in/pdf/guideline/national_health_policy_2002.pdf.

(h) National Water Policy (2002)

National water policy was a landmark development in the field of environmental protection in the country. It streamlined the importance of water management. It said, 'In view of the vital importance of water for human and animal life, for maintaining ecological balance and for economic and developmental activities of all kinds, and considering its increasing scarcity, the planning and management of this resource and its optimal, economical and equitable use has become a matter of the utmost urgency.' Concerns of the community need to be taken into account for the development and management of water resources. The success of the National Water Policy will depend entirely on evolving and maintaining a national consensus and commitment to its underlying principles and objectives. To achieve the desired objectives, State Water Policy backed with an operational action plan shall be formulated in a time-bound manner in two years.[102]

(i) Tenth Five-Year Plan (2002–2007)

Population growth and economic development were integrated with environment conservation in this plan. Various action plans for the reduction of pollution levels were incorporated into the planning. The Tenth Plan was a period of extensive review of environmental processes and laws. The first National Environment Policy was put into place in May 2006. A lot of emphasis was given on environmental educational education amongst masses through the involvement of nongovernmental organisations, youth educational institutes, and other voluntary organisations.

(j) Eleventh Five-Year Plan (2007–2012)

Faster and more inclusive growth has been the approach of the Eleventh Five-Year Plan of the government of India. The empowerment of Panchayati Raj Institutions (PRIs) was emphasised in this plan. The Eleventh Plan was aimed at putting the economy on a sustainable growth

---

[102] See National Water Policy, 2002, published by Ministry of Water, Government of India; available at http://mowr.gov.in/writereaddata/linkimages/ nwp20025617515534.pdf.

trajectory, with a growth rate of approximately 10 per cent. Productive employment was envisaged at a faster pace than before and a robust agriculture growth at 4 per cent per year. The Eleventh Plan of the government of India sought to reduce disparities across regions and communities by ensuring access to basic physical infrastructure as well as health and education services to all. It recognised gender as a cross-cutting theme across all sectors and committed to respect and promote the rights of the common person, which was a hallmark of an inclusive and sustainable growth pattern. Recognising that climate change poses a real challenge to future generations, it sought to streamline our development strategy to be sensitive to this concern.

(k) Twelfth Five-Year Plan (2012–2017)

One of the most important policy frameworks for the inclusion of sustainability concerns charted out by the government of India to date is the Twelfth Five-Year Plan. 'Economic growth and development have to be guided by the compulsion of sustainability, because none of us has the luxury, any longer, of ignoring the economic as well as the environmental threat, that a fast-deteriorating ecosystem poses to our fragile planet. None of us is immune to the reality of climate change, ecological degradation, depletion of the ozone layer and contamination of our freshwater.'[103]

For us today, the most relevant facets for the sustainability paradigm are the ideas and projections of the Twelfth Five-Year Plan of the government of India. The Twelfth Five-Year Plan has for the first time in India given the idea of estimating green national accounts, which would measure national production while allowing for the negative effects on national resources. This will be the indicator of the real gross domestic product (GDP) of the country. Corporate sustainability has been given emphasis in this plan by the union government. It comes out of two ingredients: one is eco efficiency, and another is socio efficiency. Eco efficiency is the economic value added by a firm in relation to its aggregated ecological impact. The World Business Council for Sustainable Development (WBCSD) has defined eco efficiency

---

[103] See Twelfth Five-Year Plan, 'Faster, More Inclusive, and Sustainable Growth,' Planning Commission, Government of India, 2012, New Delhi, p. 112; available at http://planningcommission.nic.in/.

as follows: 'Eco-efficiency is achieved by the delivery of competitively priced goods and services that satisfy human needs and bring quality of life, while progressively reducing ecological impacts and resource intensity throughout the life-cycle, to a level at least in line with the earth's carrying capacity.'[104]

Socio efficiency is the relation between a firm's value added and its social impact. Depending on the type of socio efficiency, a corporate entity can either try to minimise the negative social impact or maximise the positive social impact while pursuing value-added activity. For sustainable economic growth, both eco efficiency and socio efficiency are needed to be reflected in corporate social and economic responsibility.[105]

In conformity with the polluter pays principle, the idea of environmental taxes as simple and efficient financial instruments for improving the productivity of natural resources has been mooted in this plan. Instead of including environmental taxes on water and fossil fuels in its general revenues, the government should directly plough back it into environmentally sustainable action on these fronts. Coal cess is a good example of environment tax imposed by the government of India in recent times, whose proceeds are channelled to the National Clean Energy Fund. As per the Twelfth Plan document, India has taken upon itself the voluntary target of reducing the emission intensity of its GDP by 20–25 per cent, over the 2005 levels, by 2020.

For the sustainable management of the Himalayan ecosystem, The Hill Area Development Programme (HADP) needs to be continued in the Twelfth Plan with renewed vigour so that the natural resources of these fragile areas can be preserved and used in a more sustainable manner. Recognising the peculiar problems of most of the hill areas as the lack of infrastructure—particularly roads, power, educational institutions, and health care centres—suggests that the G. B. Pant Institute for Himalayan Environment and Development (GBPIHED) should reorient its activities to sustainable development and evolve as a centre of excellence and as a resource base for advice on sustainable development of the Himalayan states. Recognising the peculiarity of the sparse habitation pattern of the hill areas, the most sustainable pattern of development can only be local solutions and

---

[104] See http://www.wbcsd.org/home.aspx.

[105] Ibid.

people's participation in decision making. Socioeconomic development of the mountain habitations can only save the fragile Himalayan ecosystem. The plan wishes to start an Indian alpine. Initiative should also be taken for tracking the dynamics of alpine biomes in the context of climate change. The table below narrates the routes through which the policymakers propose to achieve sustainable development in the Indian legislations.

Table 3. Sustainability Factor Identification and Implementation Route in Twelfth Five-Year Plan (2012–2017)		
Sustainability Factor		**Implementation Route**
1.	INCLUSIVENESS	• Inclusiveness as poverty reduction • Inclusiveness as group equality • Inclusiveness as regional balance • Inclusiveness as empowerment • Inclusiveness through employment Programmes
2.	ENVIRONMENTAL SUSTAINABILITY	• Nuclear and hydro energy as an important substitute for coal-based electricity • New energy-efficient practices in urban housing and transport • A global cooperative solution for the reduction of greenhouse gases (GHGs) • A national action plan for climate change to achieve the stated objective of reducing the emissions intensity of our GDP by 20 per cent to 25 per cent between 2005 and 2020.
3.	DEVELOPING HUMAN CAPABILITIES	• Life and longevity • Education • Skill development • Nutrition • Health • Drinking water and sanitation • Enhancing human capabilities through information technology
4.	DEVELOPMENT OF INSTITUTIONAL CAPABILITIES	• Governmental decision-making systems need to be redesigned. • Delivery of public services should be made more effective. • Regulatory institutions need to be strengthened.

		• India has three pillars of governance (legislature, executive, and judiciary) and three tiers of government (centre, state, and panchayats/ULBs). The capabilities of these institutions to deliver on their mandate need to be greatly improved. • Implementation capability of governance needs to be improved.
5.	DEVELOPMENT OF INFRASTRUCTURE	• Power • Telecommunications • Road transport • Railways • Airports • Ports • Financing infrastructure through the induction of private participation in the development of infrastructure • Extending the concept of PPP to social and urban sector projects, the need for the participation of 'people' in the design and monitoring of PPP schemes becomes crucial. Local citizens are direct stakeholders in such projects, and therefore, their support becomes crucial. Therefore, we must begin to shape PPPs in the social and urban sectors as people–public–private partnerships (PPPPs) to achieve greater sustainability.
6.	MANAGING NATURAL RESOURCES AND THE ENVIRONMENT	• Soil health and productivity. • Rational use of Land • Water as a scarce natural resource
7.	ENGAGEMENT WITH THE WORLD	India's growth prospects in the years ahead cannot be viewed in isolation from what is happening in the world economy. The major industrialised and developing countries, meeting at Summit level in the G20, have repeatedly emphasised the importance of avoiding disruptive outcomes and the need for all countries to act in concert and cooperation to bring the global economy back on a path of sustainable growth.

National Enactments

Since the beginning, the Indian parliament has been very sensitive towards sustainable development principles. Legislative enactments were always coloured with principles of economic and social security. Keeping pace with international commitments, the Indian parliament passed various laws effecting and regulating environmental issues. India also gained credit as the first country that made provisions for the protection and improvement of the environment in its constitution.

By way of the forty-second amendment to the constitution in 1976, directive principles of state policy in chapter 4 of the constitution as Article 48-A was inserted, which enjoins the state to endeavour for the protection and improvement of the environment and for safeguarding the forests and wildlife of the country.

Another landmark provision in respect to the environment was also inserted, by the same amendment, as Article 51-A (g) of the constitution as one of the fundamental duties of every citizen of India. It stipulates that it shall be the duty of every citizen of India 'to protect and improve the natural environment including forests, lakes, rivers and wild life and to have compassion for living creatures'. The table below narrates some of the most important national enactments that address the issue of sustainable development.

Table 4. Important Indian Legislations in the Area of Sustainable Development	
Sustainability Area	**Legislations**
Social	• Protection of Human Rights Act, 1993 • National Trust Act, 1999 • Commissions for the Protection of Child Rights Act, 2005 • Right to Information Act, 2005 • Gram Nyayalayas Act, 2009 • Right of Children to Free and Compulsory Education Act, 2009
Economic	• Foreign Trade (Development and Regulation) Act, 1992 • Competition Act, 2002 • Fiscal Responsibility and Budget Management Act, 2003 • Micro, Small, and Medium Enterprises Development Act, 2006

Environmental	• The Forest Act, 1927 • The Wildlife (Protection) Act, 1972 • Water (Prevention and Control of Pollution) Act, 1974 • The Forest (Conservation) Act, 1980 • Air (Prevention and Control of Pollution) Act, 1981 • Environmental (Protection) Act, 1986 • Motor Vehicles Act, 1988
Socioecological (Environmental and Social)	• Public Liability Insurance Act, 1991 • National Environment Tribunal Act, 1995 (Repealed) • The National Environment Appellate Authority Act, 1997 (Repealed) • National Green Tribunal Act, 2010
Social Equity (Economic and Social)	• Person with Disabilities Act, 1995 (right of the disabled to employment) • The Geographical Indications of Goods (Registration and Protection) Act, 1999 • Protection of Plant Varieties and Farmer's Right Act, 2001 • The Patents (Amendment) Act, 2005 • Maintenance and Welfare of Parents and Senior Citizens Act, 2007
Green Economy (Economic and Environmental)	• Energy Conservation Act, 2001 • The Electricity Act, 2003
Sustainable Development (Social, Environmental, and Economic)	• The (Wildlife Protection Act), 1972 and its amendments in 1991 and 2002 • Panchayat Extension to Scheduled Areas Act, 1996 • Biological Diversity Act, 2002; and the Biological Diversity Rules, 2004 • National Rural Employment Guarantee Act, 2005 • Forests Rights Act, 2006 • National Food Security Act, 2013

CHAPTER V

JUDICIAL RESPONSE

Relaxing the Rule of *Locus Standi* by the Supreme Court of India

The social and economic well-being of the citizens have always been the core concerns of the judiciary in India. With the advent of the economic liberalisation in the Indian economy, political and social norms also underwent a change. With the rapid growth of economy, various developmental activities started; and in turn, natural resources of the country came under pressure. It was the backdrop in which the Hon'ble Supreme Court of India relaxed the traditional rule of standing (*locus standi*) and started a new era of public interest litigation. Traditionally, the rule was that the court shall hear only the matters brought by the parties who have their own stakes in the matter or, in other words, the matter brought by the parties who are themselves aggrieved by the cause of action. Most of the judicial response to the omissions and commissions of the legislature as well as the executive in the field of sustainable development jurisprudence have been corrected by way of public interest litigation by the Hon'ble Supreme Court of India. Various measures for social upliftment and the well-being of the downtrodden sections of society have been taken by the Indian courts through public interest litigation. Through public interest petitions, the courts have recognised the concept of 'representative standing' in a *lis*. Instead of an adversarial setting where the judge relies on the counsels to produce evidence and argue their cases, the PIL cases are characterised by a collaborative problem-solving approach. Acting either at the instance of petitioners or on their own, the supreme court has invoked article 32 of the constitution to grant interim remedies, such as stay orders and injunctions, to restrain harmful activities in many cases. Reliance has also been placed on those in power to do complete justice under article 142 to issue detailed guidelines to executive agencies and private parties for ensuring the implementation of various environmental statutes.[106]

---

[106] See K. G. Balakrishnan, *The Role of Judiciary in Environmental Protection*, D. P. Shrivastava memorial lecture, 2010; available at www.sci.nic.in.

In *Bandhua Mukti Morcha v. Union of India and Others*,[107] J. Pathak, while concurring, held 'public interest litigation in its present from constitutes a new chapter in our judicial system. It has acquired a significant degree of importance in the jurisprudence practised by our courts and has evoked a lively, if somewhat controversial, response in legal circles, in the media and among the general public'. In the United States, it is the name 'given to efforts to provide legal representation to groups and interests that have been unrepresented or under-represented in the legal process. These include not only the poor and the disadvantaged but ordinary citizens who, because they cannot afford lawyers to represent them, have lacked access to courts, administrative agencies and other legal forums in which basic policy decisions affecting their interests are made. In our own country, this new class of litigation is justified by its protagonists on the basis generally of vast areas in our population of illiteracy and poverty, of social and economic backwardness, and of an insufficient awareness and appreciation of individual and collective rights. These handicaps have denied millions of our countrymen access to justice. Public interest litigation is said to possess the potential of providing such access in the milieu of a new ethos, in which participating sectors in the administration of justice co-operate in the creation of a system which promises legal relief without cumbersome formality and heavy expenditure. In the result, the legal organization has taken on a radically new dimension, and correspondingly new perspectives are opening up before judges and lawyers and State law agencies in the tasks before them. A crusading zeal is abroad, viewing the present as an opportunity to awaken the political and legal order to the objectives of social justice projected in our constitutional system. New slogans fill the air, and new phrases have entered the legal dictionary, and we hear of the "justicing system" being galvanized into supplying justice to the socioeconomic disadvantaged. These urges are responsible for the birth of new judicial concepts and the expanding horizon of juridical power. They claim to represent an increasing emphasis on social welfare and progressive humanitarianism'.[108]

The apex court held that the bonded labour practice is in violation of fundamental dignity ensured to every citizen of this country through article 21 of the Constitution of India. It held that 'the Central Government is

---

[107] AIR 1984 SC 802.

[108] Ibid.

therefore bound to ensure observance of various social welfare and labour laws enacted by Parliament for the purpose of securing to the workmen a life of basic human dignity in compliance with the Directive Principles of State Policy'. In *Francis Coralie Mullin v. Union Territory of Delhi*,[109] Bhagwati J. stated, 'The right to life includes the right to live with human dignity and all that goes along with it, namely, the bare necessaries of life such as adequate nutrition, clothing and shelter and facilities for reading, writing and expressing oneself in diverse forms, freely moving about and mixing and commingling with fellow human beings. Of course, the magnitude and content of the components of this right would depend upon the extent of the economic development of the country, but it must, in any view of the matter, include the right to the basic necessities of life and also the right to carry on such functions and activities as constitute the bare minimum expression of the human-self.'[110]

In the matter of *Rural Litigation and Entitlement Kendra and Others v. State of Uttar Pradesh and Others*,[111] the Hon'ble Supreme Court, while emphasising the importance of article 51 (g) of the Constitution of India, held as the following: 'Consciousness for environmental protection is of recent origin. The United Nations Conference on World Environment held in Stockholm in June 1972 and the follow-up action thereafter is spreading the awareness. Over thousands of years men had been successfully exploiting the ecological system for his sustenance but with the growth of population the demand for land has increased and forest growth has been and is being cut down and man has started encroaching upon Nature and its assets. Scientific developments have made it possible and convenient for man to approach the places which were hitherto beyond his ken. The consequences of such be sufficient quantity of rain. The top soil may be preserved without being eroded and the natural setting of the area may remain intact. We had commended earlier to the State of Uttar Pradesh as also to the Union of India that afforestation activity may be carried out in the whole valley and the hills. We have been told that such activity has been undertaken. We are not oblivious of the fact that natural resources have got to be tapped for the purposes of social development but one cannot forget at the same time that

---

[109]   1981 (1) SCC 608.

[110]   Ibid.

[111]   AIR 1987 SC 359.

tapping of resources have to be done with requisite attention and care so that ecology and environment may not be affected in any serious way; there may not be any depletion of water resources and long-term planning must be undertaken to keep up the national wealth. It has always to be remembered that these are interference with ecology and environment have now came to be realized. It is necessary that the Himalayas and the forest growth on the mountain range should be left uninterfered with so that there may permanent assets of mankind and are not intended to be exhausted in one generation. We must place on record our appreciation of the steps taken by the Rural Litigation and Entitlement Kendra. But for this move, all that has happened perhaps may not have come. Preservation of the environment and keeping the ecological balance unaffected is a task which not only Governments but also every citizen must undertake. It is a social obligation and let us remind every Indian citizen that it is his fundamental duty as enshrined in Article 51 A (g) of the Constitution.'[112]

The concept of sustainable development contains three basic components or principles. First among these is the precautionary principle, whereby the state must anticipate, prevent, and attack the cause of environmental degradation. The Rio Declaration affirms the principle by stating that wherever 'there are threats of serious or irreversible damage, lack of full scientific certainty shall not be used as a reason for postponing cost-effective measures to prevent environmental degradation'. Most of the cases of the 1990s deal with the definition of the principle. In 1996, the supreme court stated that environmental measures adopted by the state government and the statutory authorities must anticipate, prevent, and attack the causes of environmental degradation. Following the definition provided in the Rio Declaration, the court stated that where there are threats of serious and irreversible damage, lack of scientific certainty should not be used as a reason for postponing measures to prevent environmental degradation.[113]

In the case of *Subhash Kumar v. State of Bihar and Others*,[114] Justice K. N. Singh, writing for himself and for Justice N. D. Ojha, streamlined the remedy of public interest litigation for the protection of environment and declared in the judgement as follows: 'Right to live is a fundamental right

---

[112] Ibid.

[113] Ibid.

[114] 1991 (1) SCC 598.

under Art 21 of the Constitution and it includes the right of enjoyment of pollution free water and air for full enjoyment of life. If anything endangers or impairs that quality of life in derogation of laws, a citizen has right to have recourse to Art, 32 of the Constitution for removing the pollution of water or air which may be detrimental to the quality of life. A petition under Art. 32 for the prevention of pollution is maintainable at the instance of affected persons or even by a group of social workers or journalists.'[115]

Jurisprudence on the matters of environmental protection and sustainable development was foremost discussed by Hon'ble Justice Kuldeep Singh while delivering judgement in the matter of *Vellore Citizens Welfare Forum v. Union of India and Others*.[116] In the judgement giving way to international sustainable development principles to be followed in the Indian domestic legal arena, it held the following: 'The traditional concept that development and ecology are opposed to each other, is no longer acceptable. Sustainable Development is the answer.'[117]

In the international sphere, 'sustainable development' as a concept came to be known for the first time in the Stockholm Declaration of 1972. Thereafter, in 1987, the concept was given definite shape by the World Commission on Environment and Development in its report called 'Our Common Future'. The commission was chaired by the then prime minister of Norway G. H. Brundtland, and as such, the report is popularly known as the Brundtland Report. In 1991, the World Conservation Union, United Nations Environment Programme, and World Wide Fund for Nature jointly came out with a document called 'Caring for the Earth', which is a strategy for sustainable living. Finally came the Earth Summit, held in June 1992 at Rio de Janeiro, which saw the largest gathering of world leaders ever in the history—deliberating and chalking out a blueprint for the survival of the planet. Amongst the tangible achievements of the Rio Conference was the signing of two conventions: one on biological diversity and another on climate change. These conventions were signed by 153 nations. The delegates also approved by consensus three nonbinding documents: a statement on forestry principles, a declaration of principles on environmental policy and development, and Agenda 21, a programme of action into the next century in

---

[115] Ibid.

[116] 1996 (5) SCC 647.

[117] Ibid.

areas like poverty, population, and pollution. During the two decades from Stockholm to Rio, sustainable development came to be accepted as a viable concept in eradicating poverty and improving the quality of human life while living within the carrying capacity of the supporting ecosystems. Sustainable development, as defined by the Brundtland Report, means 'development that meets the needs of the present without compromising the ability of the future generations to meet their own needs'.[118] The hon'ble court has categorically viewed that both ecology and growth are the components of sustainable development as shown below.

Figure 1. The Supreme Court's View in the
***Vellore Citizens Welfare Forum* Case**

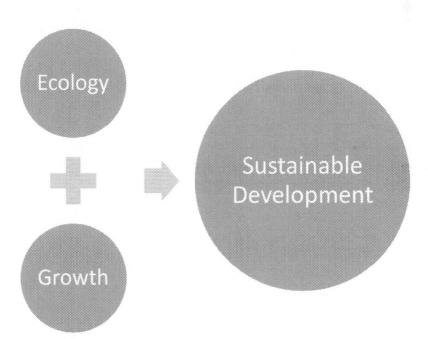

We have no hesitation in holding that sustainable development as a balancing concept between ecology and development has been accepted as part of the customary international law. However, its salient feature has yet to be finalised by international law jurists. Some of the salient

---

118   Ibid.

principles of sustainable Development, as culled out from the Brundtland Report and other international documents, are intergenerational equity, use and conservation of natural resources, environmental protection, the precautionary principle, the polluter pays principle, obligation to assist and cooperate, eradication of poverty, and financial assistance to developing countries. We are however of the view that the precautionary principle and the polluter pays principle are essential features of sustainable development. The precautionary principle, in the context of the municipal law, means the following: (i) In terms of environmental measures, by the state government and the statutory authorities, it must anticipate, prevent, and attack the causes of environmental degradation. (ii) Where there are threats of serious and irreversible damage, the lack of scientific certainty should not be used as the reason for postponing measures to prevent environmental degradation. (iii) The onus of proof is on the actor or the developer/industrialist to show that his action is environmentally benign.[119]

The Supreme Court of India has identified the principles of sustainable development law from international instruments and has from time to time incorporated them all into Indian jurisprudence. The efforts of the courts to incorporate the international principles of sustainable development law have been very fundamental to the growth of domestic sustainable development law in India. Some of them have been depicted in the figure below.

---

[119]   Ibid.

Figure 2. Sustainable Development Principles
Incorporated by the Indian Supreme Court

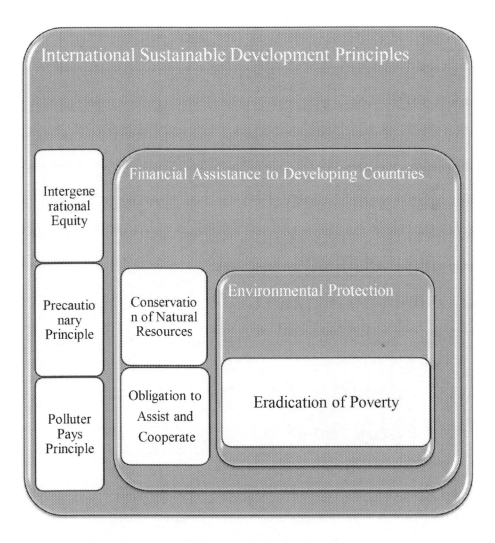

The polluter pays principle has been held to be a sound principle by this court in *Indian Council for Enviro-Legal Action v. Union of India*.[120] The court observed, 'We are of the opinion that any principle evolved in this behalf should be simple practical and suited to the conditions obtaining in this country'. The court ruled that 'once the activity carried on is hazardous

---

[120]   AIR 1996 SC 1446.

or inherently dangerous, the person carrying on such activity is liable to make good the loss caused to any other person by his activity irrespective of the fact whether he took reasonable care while carrying on his activity. The rule is premised upon the very nature of the activity carried on'.[121]

Consequently, the polluting industries are 'absolutely liable to compensate for the harm caused by them to villagers in the affected area, to the soil and to the underground water and hence, they are bound to take all necessary measures to remove sludge and other pollutants lying in the affected areas'. The polluter pays principle, as interpreted by this court, means that the absolute liability for harm to the environment extends to compensate not only the victims of pollution but also the cost of restoring environmental degradation. Remediation of the damaged environment is part of the process of sustainable development, and as such, the polluter is liable to pay the cost to the individual sufferers as well as the cost of reversing the ecological damage. The precautionary principle and the polluter pays principle have been accepted as part of the law of the land.[122]

The figure below shows the facets of the polluter pays principle recognised by the Indian Supreme Court.

Figure 3. Polluter Pays Principle Recognised by the Supreme Court

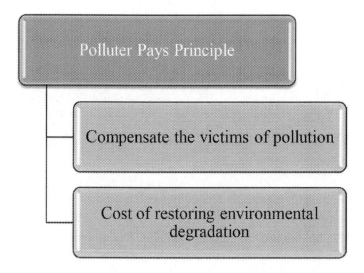

---

[121] Ibid.

[122] Ibid.

Article 21 of the Constitution of India guarantees the protection of life and personal liberty. Articles 47, 48A, and 51A (g) of the constitution are as follows:

> Article 47: Duty of the State to raise the level of nutrition and the standard of living and to improve public health. The State shall regard the raising of the level of nutrition and the standard of living of its people and the improvement of public health as among its primary duties and in particular, The State shall endeavor to bring about prohibition of the consumption except for medicinal purposes of intoxicating drinks and of drugs which are injurious to health.[123]
>
> Article 48A. (g): Protection and improvement of environment and safeguarding of forests and wild life. The State shall endeavor to protect and improve the environment and to safeguard the forests and wild life of the country.[124]
>
> 51A (g): To protect and improve the natural environment including forests, takes, rivers and wild life, and to have compassion for living creatures.[125]

Apart from the constitutional mandate to protect and improve the environment, there are plenty of post-independence legislations on the subject, but more relevant enactments for our purpose are the following: the Water (Prevention and Control of Pollution) Act, 1974 (the Water Act); the Air (Prevention and Control of Pollution) Act, 1981 (the Air Act); and the Environment Protection Act, 1986 (the Environment Act). The Water Act provides for the constitution of the Central Pollution Control Board by the central government and the constitution of one the State Pollution Control Boards by various state governments in the country. The boards function under the control of the governments concerned. The Water Act prohibits the use or streams and wells for the disposal of polluting matters. It also provides for restrictions on outlets and the discharge of effluents without obtaining

---

[123] Ibid.

[124] Ibid.

[125] Ibid.

consent from the board. Prosecution and penalties have been provided, which include imprisonment. The Air Act provides that the Central Pollution Control Board and the State Pollution Control Boards constituted under the later act shall also perform the powers and functions under the Air Act. The main function of the boards under the Air Act is to improve the quality of the air and to prevent, control, and abate air pollution in the country. We shall deal with the Environment Act in the later part of this judgement. In view of the above-mentioned constitutional and statutory provisions, we have no hesitation in holding that the precautionary principle and the polluter pays principle are part of the environmental law of the country.[126]

Even once these principles are accepted as part of the customary international law, there would be no difficulty in accepting them as part of domestic law. It is almost an accepted proposition of law that the rule of customary international law that is not contrary to the municipal law shall be deemed to have been incorporated into the domestic law and shall be followed by the courts of law. To support, we may refer to Justice H. R. Khanna's opinion in *Addl. Distt. Magistrate Jabalpur v. Shivakant Shukla* (AIR 1976 SC 1207), *Jolly George Varghese's* case (AIR 1980 SC 470), and *Gramophone Company's* case (AIR 1984 SC 667).[127]

The constitutional and statutory provisions protect a person's right to fresh air, clean water, and a pollution-free environment; but the source of the right is the inalienable common law right of a clean environment. It would be useful to quote a paragraph from Blackstone's commentaries on the laws of England (*Commentaries on the Laws of England* by Sir William Blackstone, vol. 3, fourth edition, published in 1876). Chapter 8, 'Of Nuisance', depicts the law on the subject in the following words: 'Also, if a person keeps his hogs, or other noisome animals, or allows filth to accumulate on his premises, so near the house of another, that the stench incommodes him and makes the air unwholesome, this is an injurious nuisance, as it tends to deprive him of the use and benefit of his house. A like injury is, if one's neighbour sets up and exercises any offensive trade; as a tanner's, a tallow chandler's, or the like; for though these are lawful and necessary trades, yet they should be exercised in remote places; for the rule is, *sic utere tuo, ut alienum non laedas*; this therefore is an actionable nuisance. And on a similar principle

---

[126]   *Ibid.*

[127]   *Ibid.*

a constant ringing of bells in one's immediate neighborhood may be a nuisance, it is a nuisance to stop or divert water that used to run to another's meadow or mill; to corrupt or poison a water-course, by erecting a due house or a lime-pit, for the use of trade, in the upper part of the stream; to pollute a pond. from which another is entitled to water his cattle: to obstruct a drain; or in short to do any act in common property, that in its consequences must necessarily tend to the prejudice of one's neighbour. So closely does the law of England enforce that excellent rule of gospel-morality, of "doing to others as we would they should do unto ourselves." Our legal system having been founded on the British Common law the right of a person to pollution free environment is a part of the basic jurisprudence of the land.'[128]

In *Chameli Singh v. State of UP,*[129] the Hon'ble Apex Court interpreted article 21 of the Constitution of India in the light of sustainability jurisprudence in the following words: 'Right to live, guaranteed in any civilized society implies the right to food, water, decent environment education, medical care and shelter. These are basic human rights known to any civilized society. All civil, political, social and cultural rights enshrined in the Universal Declaration of Human Rights and Convention or under the Constitution of India cannot be exercised without these basic human rights. Shelter for a human being, therefore, is not a mere protection of his life and limb.'[130]

In *CESC Ltd. v. Subhash Chandra Bose,*[131] the Hon'ble Supreme Court held the following: 'Right to social and economic justice is a fundamental right. Right to health of a worker is a fundamental right. Therefore, right to life enshrined in Article 21 means something more than mere survival of animal existence. The right to live with human dignity with minimum sustenance and shelter and all those rights and aspects of life which would go to make a man's life complete and worth living, would form part of the right to life. Enjoyment of life and its attainment—social, cultural and intellectual—without which life cannot be meaningful, would embrace the protection and preservation of life guaranteed by Article 21. The State owes

---

[128] Ibid.

[129] 1996 (2) SCC 549.

[130] Ibid.

[131] 1992 (1) SCC 441.

to the homeless people to ensure at least minimum shelter as part of the State obligation under Article 21.'[132]

In the case of *M. C. Mehta v. Union of India*,[133] (Taj Trapezium matter), once again, Justice Kuldeep Singh of the Hon'ble Supreme Court of India in his judgement delivered various measures for the safety and security of the Taj Mahal, considering it a cultural heritage of great value, saying, 'The old concept that development and ecology cannot go together is no longer acceptable. Sustainable development is the answer. The development of industry is essential for the economy of the country, but at the same time the environment and the eco-systems have to be protected. The pollution created as a consequence of development must commensurate with the carrying capacity of our eco-systems.'[134]

In *Indian Council for Enviro-Legal Action v. Union of India*,[135] the Hon'ble Supreme Court held, 'With rapid industrialization taking place, there is an increasing threat to the maintenance of the ecological balance. The general public is becoming aware of the need to protect environment. Even though, laws have been passed for the protection of environment, the enforcement of the same has been tardy, to say the least. With the governmental authorities not showing any concern with the enforcement of the said Acts, and with the development taking place for personal gains at the expense of environment and with disregard of the mandatory provisions of law, some public-spirited persons have been initiating public interest litigations. The legal position relating to the exercise of jurisdiction by the courts for preventing environmental degradation and thereby, seeking to protect the fundamental rights of the citizens, is now well settled by various decisions of this Court. The primary effort of the court, while dealing with the environmental-related issues, is to see that the enforcement agencies, whether it is the State or any other authority, take effective steps for the enforcement of the laws. The courts, in a way, act as the guardian of the people's fundamental rights but in regard to many technical matters, the courts may not be fully equipped. Perforce, it has to rely on outside agencies for reports and recommendations whereupon orders have been passed from time to time. Even though, it is not

---

[132] Ibid.

[133] AIR 1997 SC 734.

[134] Ibid.

[135] 1996 (5) SCC 281.

the function of the court to see the day-to-day enforcement of the law, that being the function of the Executive, but because of the non-functioning of the enforcement agencies, the courts as of necessity have had to pass orders directing the enforcement agencies to implement the law.' [136]

The hon'ble court further observed that 'environmental law has now become a specialized field. In the decision which was taken at the United Nations Conference on Environment and Development held at Rio de Janeiro in June 1992 in which India had also participated, the States had been called upon to develop national laws regarding liability and compensation for the victims of pollution and other environmental damages'.[137]

In *A. P. Pollution Control Board II v. Prof. M. V. Nayudu (Retd.) and Others*,[138] Justice M. Jagannadha Rao adopted the resolution of the UNO passed during the United Nations Water Conference in 1977 in the Indian sustainable development law jurisprudence and confirmed the access for clean drinking water as the duty of the state, stating, 'Drinking water is of primary importance in any country.' In fact, India is a party to the resolution of the UNO passed during the United Nations Water Conference in 1977: 'All people, whatever their stage of development and their social and economic conditions, have the right to have access to drinking water in quantum and of a quality equal to their basic needs.' Thus, the right to access to drinking water is fundamental to life, and there is a duty on the state under article 21 to provide clean drinking water to its citizens.[139]

In *T. N. Godavarman Thirumalpad v. Union of India and Others*,[140] Justice Arijit Pasayat, writing for himself and for Justice B. N. Kirpal and Justice Y. K. Sabharwal, while describing the environment and the beauty of the whole idea of ecological preservation, elaborately quoted the famous story from the year 1854 about a discussion between the wise Indian chief of Seattle and the great white chief in Washington regarding the sale/purchase of the land. The court held, 'The seminal issue involved is whether the approach should be "dollar friendly" or "eco friendly".'[141]

---

[136]   Ibid.

[137]   Ibid.

[138]   2001 (2) SCC 62.

[139]   Ibid.

[140]   AIR 2003 SC 724.

[141]   Ibid.

Figure 4. Economy v. Ecology Dichotomy
Identified by the Supreme Court

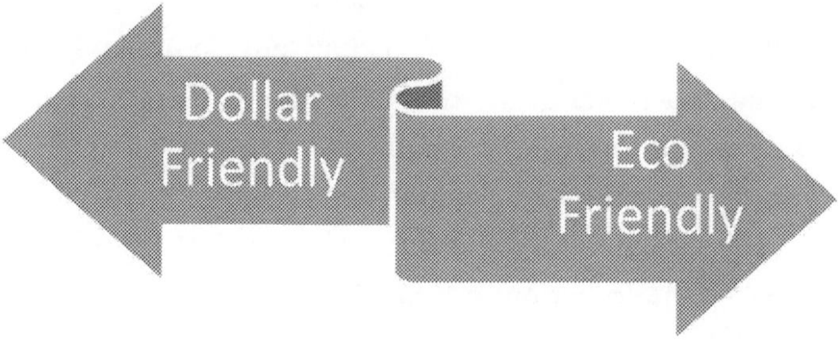

'Environment' is a difficult word to define. Its normal meaning relates to the surroundings, but obviously, that is a concept that is relatable to whatever object it is which is surrounded. Einstein had once observed, 'The environment is everything that isn't me.' About one and half century ago, in 1854, as the famous story goes, the wise Indian chief of Seattle replied to the offer of the great white chief in Washington to buy their land. The reply is profound. It is beautiful. It is timeless. It contains the wisdom of the ages. It is the first ever and the most understanding statement on the environment. The whole of it is worth quoting, as any extract from it is to destroy its beauty.[142]

> How can you buy or sell the sky, the warmth of the land? The idea is strange to us. If we do not own the freshness of the air and the sparkle of the water, how can you buy them? Every part of the earth is sacred to my people. Every shining pine needle, every sandy shore, every mist in the dark woods, every clearing and humming insect is holy in the memory and experience of my people. The sap which courses through the trees carries the memories of the red man. 'the white man's dead forget the country of their birth when they go to walk among the stars. Our dead never forget this beautiful earth, for it is the mother of the red man. We are part of the earth and it is part of us. The perfumed flowers are our sisters; the horse, the great eagle, these are our brothers. The rocky crests, the juices in

---

[142] Ibid.

the meadows, the body heat of the pony, and man—all belong to the same family.' So, when the Great Chief in Washington sends word and he wishes to buy our land, he asks much of us. The Great Chief sends word he will reserve us a place so that we can live comfortably to ourselves. He will be our father and we will be his children. So we will consider your offer to buy land. But it will not be easy. For this land is sacred to us. This shining water moves is the streams and rivers is not just water but the blood of our ancestors. If we sell you land, you must remember that it is sacred, and you must teach your children that it is sacred and that each ghostly reflection in the clear water of the lakes tells of events and memories in the life of my people. The water's murmur is the voice of my father's father. The rivers are our brothers, they quench our thirst. The rivers carry our canoes, and feed our children. If we sell you our land you must remember, and teach your children, that the rivers are our brothers, and yours and you must henceforth give the kindness you would give any brother. We know that the white man does not understand our ways. One portion of land is the same to him as the next, for he is a stranger who comes in the night and takes from the land whatever he needs. The earth is not his brother but this enemy and when he has conquered it, he moves on. He leaves his father's graves behind, and he does not care. He kidnaps the earth from his children. His father's grave and his children's birthright are forgotten. He treats his mother, the earth, and his brother, the sky, as things to be bought, plundered, sold like sheep or bright beads. His appetite will devour the earth and leave behind only a desert. I do not know. Our ways are different from your ways. The sight of your cities pains the eyes of the red man. But perhaps it is because the red man is a savage and does not understand. There is no quite place in the white man's cities. No place to hear the unfurling of leaves in spring or the rustle of in insect's wings. But perhaps it is because I am a savage and do not understand. The clatter only seems to insult the ears. And what is there in life if a man cannot hear the lonely cry of the whippoorwill or the arguments of the frogs around a pond at night? I am a red man and do not understand. The Indian prefers the soft sound of the wind darting over the face of a pond, and the smell of the wind itself, cleansed by a mid-day rain, or scented with the pinon pine. The air is precious to the red man, for all things share the same breath—the beast, the tree, the man, they all share the same breath. The white man does not seem to notice the air he breathes. Like a man lying for many days, he is numb to the stench. But if we sell you our land, you must remember that the air is precious to us, that the air shares its spirit with all the life it supports. The wind that gave our grandfather his first breath also receives the last sign. And if we sell you our land, you must keep it apart and sacred as a place where even the white man can go to taste the wind that is sweetened by the meadow's flowers. So we will consider your offer to buy our land. If we decide to accept, I will make one condition. The white man must treat the beasts of this land as his brothers. I am a savage and I do not understand any other way. I have seen thousand rotting buffaloes on the prairie, left by the white man who shot them from a passing train. I am a savage and I do not understand how the smoking iron horse can be more important than the buffalo that we kill only to stay alive. What is man without the beasts? If all the beasts were gone, man would die from a great loneliness of spirit. For whatever happens to the beasts soon happens to man. All things are connected. You must teach your children that the ground beneath their feet is the ashes of our grandfathers, so that they will respect the land. Tell your children that the earth is rich with the lives of our kin. Teach your children what we have taught our children that the earth is our mother. Whatever befalls the earth befalls the sons of the earth. If man spit upon the ground, they spit upon themselves. This we know: The earth does not belong to man, man belongs to the earth. This we know: All things are connected like the blood which unites one family. All things are connected. Whatever befalls the earth befalls the sons of the earth. Man did not wave the web of life; he is merely a stand in it. Whatever he does to the web he does to himself. Even the white man, whose God walks and talks with him as friend to friend cannot be exempt from the common destiny. We may be brothers after all. We shall see. One thing we know, which the white man may one day discover—our God is the same God. You may think now that you own him as you wish to own our land; but you cannot.

He is the God of man, and his compassion is equal for the red man and the white. This earth is precious to him, and to harm the earth is to heap contempt on the creator. The white too shall pass perhaps sooner than all other tribes. Contaminate your bed and you will one night suffocate in your own waste. But in your perishing you will shine brightly, fired by the strength of the God who brought you this land and for some special purpose gave you dominion over this land and over the red man. That destiny is a mystery to us, for we do not understand when the wild buffaloes are slaughtered, the wild horses are tamed, the secret corners of the forest heavy with scent of many men and the view of the hills blotted by talking wires. Where is the thicket? Gone, where is the eagle? Gone. The end of living and the beginning of survival.[143]

The hon'ble court further mandated that 'to protect and improve the environment is a constitutional mandate. It is a commitment for a country wedded to the ideas of a welfare State. The world is under an impenetrable cloud. In view of enormous challenges thrown by the Industrial revolution, the legislatures throughout the world are busy in their exercise to find out means to protect the world. Every individual in the society has a duty to protect the nature. People worship the objects of nature. The trees, water, land and animals had gained important positions in the ancient times. As Manu VIII, page 282 says different punishments were prescribed for causing injuries to plants. Kautilya went a step further and fixed the punishment on the basis of importance of the part of the tree'.[144]

In *N. D. Jayal and Another v. Union of India and Others*,[145] Hon'ble Supreme Court of India, while deciding the issues relating to the construction of the Tehri Hydropower Project, also deliberated upon the concept of sustainable development: 'The right to development cannot be treated as a mere right to economic betterment or cannot be limited to as misnomer to simple construction activities. The right to development encompasses much more than economic well being, and includes within its definition the guarantee of fundamental human rights. The "development" is not

---

[143] Ibid.

[144] Ibid.

[145] AIR 2004 SC 867.

related only to the growth of GNP. In the classic work "Development as Freedom" the Nobel prize winner Amartya Sen pointed out that "the issue of development cannot be separated from the conceptual framework of human right". This idea is also part of the UN Declaration on the Right to Development. The right to development includes the whole spectrum of civil, cultural, economic, political and social process, for the improvement of people's well being and realization of their full potential. It is an integral part of human right. Of course, construction of a dam or a mega project is definitely an attempt to achieve the goal of wholesome development. Such works could very well be treated as integral component for development. Therefore, the adherence of sustainable development principle is a sine qua non for the maintenance of the symbiotic balance between the rights to environment and development. Right to environment is a fundamental right. On the other hand right to development is also one. Here the right to "sustainable development" is to be treated an integral part of "life" under Article 21.'[146]

Weighty concepts like intergenerational equity (*State of Himachal Pradesh v. Ganesh Wood Products*, 1995 [6] SCC 363), public trust doctrine (*M. C. Mehta v. Kamal Nath*, 1997 [1] SCC 383), and precautionary principle (*Vellore Citizens*), which we declared as inseparable ingredients of our environmental jurisprudence, could only be nurtured by ensuring sustainable development.[147]

Further declaring the principles of sustainable development as the hallmark of the Constitution of India, Justice Ruma Pal in her judgement in the matter of *Essar Oil Limited v. Halar Utkarsh Samiti and Others*[148] held the following: 'In our opinion this must be done keeping in mind the Stockholm Declaration of 1972 which has been described as the "Magna-Carta of our environment". Indeed in the wake of the Stockholm Declaration in 1972, as far as this country is concerned, provisions to protect the environment were incorporated in the Constitution by an amendment in 1976. Article 48A of the Constitution now provides that the "State shall endeavour to protect and improve the environment and to safeguard the forests and wildlife of the country". It is also now one of the fundamental duties of

---

[146] *Ibid.*

[147] *Ibid.*

[148] 2004 (2) SCC 392.

every citizen of the country under Article 51A (g) "to protect and improve the natural environment including forests, lakes, rivers and wildlife and to have compassion for living creatures".[149] Certain principles were enunciated in the Stockholm Declaration giving broad parameters and guidelines for the purposes of sustaining humanity and its environment. Of these parameters, a few principles are extracted which are of relevance to the present debate. Principle 2 provides that the natural resources of the earth including the air, water, land, flora and fauna especially representative samples of natural ecosystems must be safeguarded for the benefit of present and future generations through careful planning and management as appropriate.'[150]

In the same vein, the fourth principle says 'man has special responsibility to safeguard and wisely manage the heritage of wild life and its habitat which are now gravely imperiled by a combination of adverse factors. Nature conservation including wild life must, therefore, receive importance in planning for economic developments'. These two principles highlight the need to factor in environmental considerations while providing for economic development. The need for economic development has been dealt with in principle 8, where it said that 'economic and social development is essential for ensuring a favourable living and working environment for man and for creating conditions on earth that are necessary for improvement of the quality of life'. The importance of maintaining a balance between economic development on the one hand and environmental protection on the other is again emphasised in principle 11 which says, 'The environmental policies of all States should enhance and not adversely affect the present or future development potential of developing countries nor should they hamper the attainment of better living conditions for all.'[151] From time to time, the Supreme Court of India has identified and incorporated the below-mentioned international principles in its various judgements.

---

[149]   Ibid.
[150]   Ibid.
[151]   Ibid.

**Figure 5. Principles of Stockholm Declaration
Recognised by the Supreme Court of India**

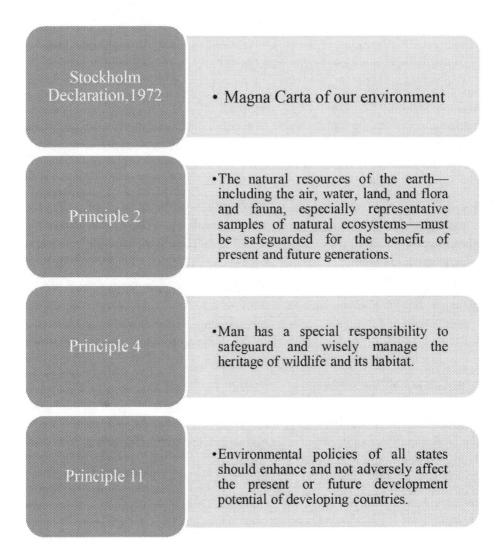

This, therefore, is the aim—namely to balance economic and social needs on the one hand with environmental considerations on the other. But in a sense, all development is an environmental threat. Indeed, the very existence of humanity and the rapid increase in population, together with consequential demands to sustain the population, have resulted in the concreting of open lands, cutting down of forests, filling up of lakes, and pollution of water resources and the very air we breathe. However, there need not necessarily be a deadlock between development on the one hand and the environment on the other. The objective of all laws on the environment should be to create harmony between the two since neither one can be sacrificed at the altar of the other.[152]

In the matter of *Intellectuals Forum, Tirupathi v. State of Andhra Pradesh and Others*,[153] Hon'ble Justice Dr. A. R. Lakshmanan, while granting leave in the special leave petition, specifically observed that the present case raises important questions at a jurisprudential level; it falls on this court to lay down the law regarding the use of public lands or natural resources that have a direct link to the environment of a particular area by the government. The hon'ble judge observed, 'The issues presented in this case illustrate the classic struggle between those members of the public who would preserve our rivers, forests, parks and open lands in their pristine purity and those charged with administrative responsibility, who under the pressures of the changing needs of an increasingly complex society find it necessary to encroach to some extent upon open lands heretofore considered inviolate to change. The resolution of this conflict in any given case is for the legislature and not for the Courts. If there is a law made by Parliament or the State Legislatures, the Courts can serve as an instrument for determining legislative intent in the exercise of powers of judicial review under the Constitution. But, in the absence of any legislation, the executive acting under the doctrine of public trust cannot abdicate the natural resource and convert them into private ownership or commercial use. The aesthetic use and the pristine glory of the natural resources, the environment and the ecosystems of our country cannot be permitted to be eroded for private, commercial or any other use unless the Courts find it necessary, in good faith, for the public and in public interest to encroach upon the said recourses.'[154]

The responsibility of the state to protect the environment is now a well-accepted notion in all countries. It is this notion that, in international law, gave rise to the principle of 'state responsibility' for pollution emanating within one's own territories (*Corfu Channel* Case, ICJ Reports, 1949 [4]). This

---

[152] Ibid.

[153] AIR 2006 (SC) 1350.

[154] Ibid.

responsibility is clearly enunciated in the 1972 United Nations Conference on the Human Environment in Stockholm (Stockholm Convention), to which India was a party. The relevant clause of this declaration in the present context is paragraph 2, which states, 'The natural resources of the earth, including the air, water, land, flora and fauna and especially representative samples of natural ecosystems, must be safeguarded for the benefit of present and future generations through careful planning or management, as appropriate.'[155]

Thus, there is no doubt about the fact that there is a responsibility bestowed upon the government to protect and preserve the tanks, which are an important part of the environment of the area. The respondents, however, have taken the plea that the actions taken by the government were in pursuance of urgent needs of development. The debate between the developmental and economic needs and that of the environment is an enduring one since if the environment is destroyed for any purpose without a compelling developmental cause, it will most probably run foul of the executive and judicial safeguards. However, this court has often faced situations where the needs of environmental protection have been pitched against the demands of economic development. In response to this difficulty, policymakers and judicial bodies across the world have produced the concept of sustainable development. This concept is defined in the 1987 report of the World Commission on Environment and Development (Brundtland Report) as 'development that meets the needs of the present without compromising the ability of the future generations to meet their own needs'.[156]

Holding sustainable development and inclusive growth as part of article 21 of the Constitution of India in the matter of *Glanrock Estate (Pvt.) Ltd. v. State of Tamil Nadu*,[157] a full bench of Justices S. H. Kapadia, Swatanter Kumar, and K. S. Radhakrishnan while deliberating on the concept of equality and inclusive growth declared the doctrine of sustainable development an integral part of the right to life enshrined under article 21 of the Constitution of India and held the following:

---

[155] Ibid.

[156] Ibid.

[157] Writ Petition (Civil) No. 242 of 1988, Supreme Court of India; available at www. sci.nic.in.

Figure 6. Supreme Court Held Sustainable Development as Part of Article 21

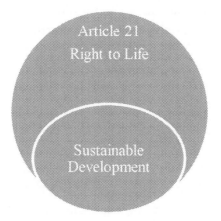

In the case of ***T. N. Godavarman v. Union of India***,[158] it has been held that intergenerational equity is part of article 21 of the constitution.[159]

Figure 7. Supreme Court Held Intergenerational Equity as Part of Article 21

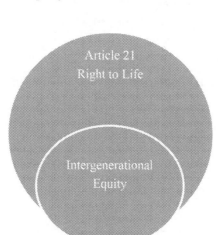

---

[158]   Writ Petition No. 202 of 1995, Supreme Court of India; available at www.sci.nic.in.

[159]   Ibid.

What is intergenerational equity? The present generation is answerable to the next generation by giving to the next generation a good environment. We are answerable to the next generation, and if deforestation takes place rampantly, then intergenerational equity would stand violated. The doctrine of sustainable development also forms part of article 21 of the constitution. The precautionary principle and the polluter pays principle flow from the core value in article 21. The important point to be noted is that in this case, we are concerned with vesting of forests in the state. When we talk about intergenerational equity and sustainable development, we are elevating an ordinary principle of equality to the level of an overarching principle. The equality doctrine has various facets. It is in this sense that in I. R. Coelho's case, this court has read article 21 with article 14. The above example indicates that when it comes to the preservation of forests as well as the environment vis-à-vis development, one has to look at the constitutional amendment not from the point of view of formal equality or equality enshrined in article 14, but on a much wider platform of an egalitarian equality, which includes the concept of inclusive growth. It is in that sense that this court has used the expression of article 21 read with article 14 in I. R. Coelho's case.[160]

The Hon'ble High Court of Madras in the matter of *Ramgopal Estates Private Limited v. State of Tamil Nadu and Others*,[161] elaborating the principles of sustainable development in its judgement, held the following: 'Right to healthy environment is the legitimate expectation, an aspect protected under Article 14 of the Constitution of India. Right to healthy environment is also a part of right to life protected under Article 21 of the Constitution of India.'[162]

---

[160] Ibid.
[161] 2007 INDLAW MAD 964.
[162] Ibid.

Figure 8. Golden/Sustainability Triangle
Recognised by the Supreme Court of India

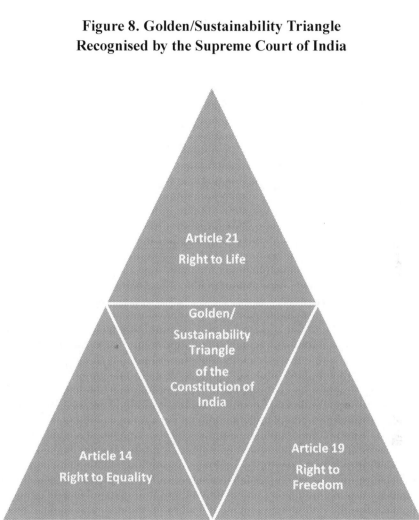

The 'first generation' rights are generally political rights, such as those found in the International Covenant on Civil and Political Rights. The 'second generation' rights are social and economic rights as found in the International Covenant on Economics, Social, and Cultural Rights. The 'third generation' rights, in today's emerging jurisprudence, encompass a group of collective rights, demanding rights to a healthy environment and giving rise to the principle of the state's responsibility to protect the environment. This responsibility is clearly enunciated in the 1972 United National Conference on the Human Environment in Stockholm (Stockholm Convention), to which India was a party (vide *Intellectual Forum v. State of AP*).[163] There is no doubt about the fact that there is a responsibility bestowed upon the government to protect and preserve the environment, as undoubtedly, a hygienic environment is an integral facet of the right to a healthy life; and it would be impossible to live without a humane and healthy environment (vide *Godavarman v. Thirumal Pad, Tamil Nadu*).[164]

While the right to a clean environment is a guaranteed fundamental right under articles 14 and 21 of the Constitution of India, the right to development through industrialisation equally claims priority under fundamental rights, particularly under articles 14, 19, and 21. Therefore, there is a necessity for sustainable development harmonising both needs and striking a golden balance between the right to development and the right to a clean environment. A concept of sustainable development is an integral part of articles 14 and 21 of the constitution (vide *N. D. Jayal v. Union of India*).[165] Before proceeding further, a sharp and detailed reference on the concept of sustainable development is inevitable.

The Stockholm Conference of 1972 refers to intergenerational equity:

- Principle 1: Man has the fundamental right to freedom, equality, and adequate conditions of life in an environment of quality that permits a life of dignity and well-being; and he bears a solemn responsibility to protect and improve the environment for the present and future generations.
- Principle 2: The natural resources of the earth, including the air, water, lands, flora and fauna, and especially representative samples of natural ecosystems must be safeguarded for the benefit of the present and future generations through careful planning or management, as appropriate.[166]

Several international conventions and treaties have recognised the above principles; and in fact, several imaginative proposals have been submitted, including the *locus standi* of individuals or groups to take action

---

[163] 2006 (3) SCC 549.
[164] 2002 (10) SCC 606.
[165] 2004 (9) SCC 362.
[166] Ibid.

as representatives of future generations or appointing an ombudsman to take care of the rights of the future against the present.[167]

The inadequacies of science result from the identification of adverse effects of a hazard and then working backwards to find the causes. Second, clinical tests are performed, particularly where toxins are involved, on animals and not on humans—that is to say, they are based on animal studies or short-term cell testing. Third, conclusions based on epidemiological studies are flawed by the scientist's inability to control or even accurately assess past exposure of the subjects. Moreover, these studies do not permit the scientist to isolate the effects of the substance of concern. It is the above uncertainty of science in the environmental context that has led international conferences to formulate new legal theories and rules of evidence. The 'uncertainty' of scientific proof and its changing frontiers from time to time have led to great changes in environmental concepts during the period between the Stockholm Conference of 1972 and the Rio Conference of 1992.[168]

The principle of precaution involves the anticipation of environmental harm and taking measures to avoid it or to choose the least environmentally harmful activity. It is based on scientific uncertainty. Environmental protection should aim at protecting not only health, property, and economic interest but also the environment for its own sake. Precautionary duties must be triggered by not only the suspicion of concrete danger but also by (justified) concern or risk potential. The precautionary principle was recommended by the UNEP Governing Council (1989). However, summing up the legal status of the precautionary principle, one commentator characterised the principle as still 'evolving', for though it is accepted as part of international customary law, 'the consequences of its application in any potential situation will be influenced by the circumstances of each case'.[169]

The traditional concept that development and ecology are opposed to each other is no longer acceptable. Sustainable development is the answer. In the international sphere, sustainable development as a concept came to be known for the first time in the Stockholm Declaration of 1972. Thereafter, in 1987, the concept was given definite shape by the World Commission on Environment and Development in its report called 'Our Common Future'.

---

[167]   Ibid.

[168]   Ibid.

[169]   Ibid.

The commission was chaired by the then prime minister of Norway G. H. Brundtland, and as such, the report is popularly known as Brundtland Report. [170]

In 1991, the World Conservation Union, United Nations Environment Programme, and World Wide Fund for Nature jointly came out with a document called 'Caring for the Earth', which is a strategy for sustainable living. Finally came the Earth Summit, held in June 1992 at Rio de Janeiro, which saw the largest gathering of world leaders ever in the history— deliberating and chalking out a blueprint for the survival of the planet. Among the tangible achievements of the Rio Conference was the signing of two conventions: one on biological diversity and another on climate change. These conventions were signed by 153 nations. The delegates also approved by consensus three nonbinding documents: a statement on forestry principles, a declaration of principles on environmental policy and development initiatives, and Agenda 21, a programme of action into the next century focused on areas like poverty, population, and pollution. Earlier, the concept was based on the 'assimilative capacity' rule as revealed in principle 6 of the 1972 Stockholm Declaration of the UN Conference on Human Environment.[171]

The said principle assumed that science could provide policymakers with the information and means necessary to avoid encroaching upon the capacity of the environment to assimilate impacts, and it presumed that relevant technical expertise would be available when environmental harm was predicted, and there would be sufficient time to act in order to avoid such harm. But in the principle 11 of the UN General Assembly resolution on World Charter for Nature of 1982, the emphasis shifted to the 'precautionary principle'; and this was reiterated in the Rio Conference of 1992 in its principle 15: 'In order to protect the environment, the precautionary approach shall be widely applied by States according to their capabilities. Where there are threats of serious or irreversible damage, lack of full scientific certainty shall not be used as a reason for proposing cost-effective measures to prevent environmental degradation.' During the two decades from Stockholm to Rio, sustainable Development has come to be accepted as a viable concept in eradicating poverty and improving the quality of human life while living

---

[170]   Ibid.

[171]   Ibid.

within the carrying capacity of the supporting ecosystems. Sustainable development, as defined by the Brundtland Report, means 'development that meets the needs of the present without compromising the ability of the future generations to meet their own needs'.[172]

Sustainable development, therefore, is a balancing concept between ecology and development. It has been accepted as part of the customary international law, though its salient features have yet to be finalised by international law jurists. Some of the salient principles of sustainable development, as culled out from the Brundtland Report and other international documents, are intergenerational equity, use and conservation of natural resources, environmental protection, the precautionary principle, the polluter pays principle, obligation to assist and cooperate, eradication of poverty, and financial assistance to developing countries. In *Vellore Citizens' Welfare Forum v. Union of India*, a three-judge bench of the apex court referred to the precautionary principle in environmental matters. J. Kuldip Singh, after referring to the principles evolved from various international conferences and the concept of sustainable development, stated that the precautionary principle, the polluter pays principle, and the special concept of onus of proof have now emerged and govern the law in our country too, as is clear from articles 47, 48A, and 51A (g) of our constitution. In fact, in various environmental statutes, including the Water Act of 1974, these concepts are already implied. These principles have now become part of our law.[173]

Thus, it was held that the precautionary principle and the polluter pays principle are essential features of sustainable development. The precautionary principle, in the context of the municipal law, means the following: (i) In terms of environmental measures, by the state government and statutory authorities, it must anticipate, prevent, and attack the causes of environmental degradation. (ii) Where there are threats of serious and irreversible damage, the lack of scientific certainty should not be used as a reason for postponing measures to prevent environmental degradation. (iii) The onus of proof is on the actor or the developer/industrialist to show that his action is environmentally benign. (xi) The polluter pays principle has been held to be a sound principle by the apex court in *Indian Council for Enviro-Legal Action v. Union of India*. The court observed, 'We are of the

---

[172]   Ibid.

[173]   Ibid.

opinion that any principle evolved in this behalf should be simple, practical and suited to the conditions obtaining this country.' The apex court observed that 'once the activity carried on is hazardous or inherently dangerous, the person carrying on such activity is liable to make good the loss caused to any other person by his activity irrespective of the fact whether he took reasonable care while carrying on his activity. The rule is premised upon the very nature of the activity carried on'. Consequently, the polluting industries are absolutely liable to compensate the villagers in the affected area for the harm they've caused to the soil and underground water; hence, they are bound to take all necessary measures to remove sludge and other pollutants lying in the affected areas. The polluter pays principle, as interpreted by this court, means that the absolute liability for harm to the environment extends to compensate not only the victims of pollution but also the cost of restoring environmental degradation. Remediation of the damaged environment is part of the process of sustainable development, and as such, the polluter is liable to pay the cost to the individual sufferers as well as the cost of reversing the damaged ecology. The precautionary principle and the polluter pays principle have been accepted as part of the law of the land. Article 21 of the Constitution of India guarantees the protection of life and personal liberty.[174]

In *Vedanta Aluminum Limited v. Union of India and others*,[175] a full bench of the Supreme Court of India declared that 'adherence to the principle of Sustainable Development is now a constitutional requirement. How much damage to the environment and ecology has got to be decided on the facts of each case. While applying the principle of Sustainable Development one must bear in mind that development which meets the needs of the present without compromising the ability of the future generations to meet their own needs is Sustainable Development. Therefore, courts are required to balance development needs with the protection of the environment and ecology. It is the duty of the State under our Constitution to devise and implement a coherent and co-ordinated programme to meet its obligation of Sustainable Development based on inter-generational equity'.[176]

A ratio of this case was recently incorporated, emphasised on, and implemented by the Uttarakhand High Court in the case of *Matri Sadan*

---

[174] AIR 2006 (SC) 1350.

[175] 2008 (2) SCC 222.

[176] Ibid.

through Its Trustees and Others v. Himalaya Stone Crusher Private Limited and Others.[177] Hon'ble Justice Servesh Kumar Gupta, writing for himself and Chief Justice Barin Ghosh, declared that 'every citizen has right to fresh air and to live in pollution free environment'. While ordering the closure of the giant stone crushers operating in a near vicinity of the human settlement, the court very strongly emphasised the need for a clean and healthy environment. Also touching upon the locus of the petitioner, the hon'ble court appreciated the efforts of the petitioner for a clean and healthy environment and observed the following: 'This Matra Sadan's Saint has resisted for running of this crusher in order to advance the duty cast upon the State by Article 51(a) (g) of the Constitution which envisages that it is the duty of every citizen of the India to protect and improve the National Environment including forests, lakes, rivers, wildlife and to have compassion for living creatures.' This fundamental duty has been inserted in the constitution by way of its popular forty-second amendment of 1976. The Hon'ble Apex Court has reiterated these duties of the citizen in a number of judgements like that of *State of Bihar v. Kedar Sao*[178] as well as *Sri M. C. Mehta v. Union of India.*[179] This way, if any citizen takes the lead in society in order to further the objective as envisaged by Article 51A (g) referred as above, then it should be appreciable and complementary by society at large.[180] The court appreciated the petitioner's consciousness towards his fundamental duty of the protection and preservation of the environment and ecology. Further, reaffirming the concept of equality as a fundamental character of the concept of sustainable development, the court gave priority to social interest and ecology over the profit motives of any individual, stating, 'We have discussed a number of deleterious affects which this stone crusher is causing to the entire of its surrounding to the extent of being fatal for the poor villagers besides creating an incorrigible hazard affects to the ecology of the region so we opine that in these circumstances, as adumbrated in the body of the judgment, the preservation of the interest of the society at large should take priority as against the profit hunting motives of any individual. Thus, this way, this

---

[177]   2011 INDLAW UTT 662

[178]   2003 INDLAW SC 651.

[179]   1997 (3) SCC 715.

[180]   2007 INDLAW MAD 964.

Court will pave the true spirit of Article 19(1) (g) of the Indian Constitution as has been done by judgment of the Hon'ble Apex Court time and again.'[181]

In *Milk Producers Association, Orissa and Others v. State of Orissa and Others*,[182] Justice S. B. Sinha, writing for himself and Justice P. K. Balasubramanyan, elevated the right to a healthy environment to the status of fundamental right, saying, 'Right to environment is a fundamental right. On the other hand, right to development is also one. Here the right to "sustainable development" cannot be singled out. Therefore, the concept of "sustainable development" is to be treated as an integral part of "life" under Article 21. Weighty concepts like intergenerational equity (State of H. P. v. Ganesh Wood Products), public trust doctrine (M. C. Mehta v. Kamal Nath) and precautionary principle (Vellore Citizens), which we declared as inseparable ingredients of our environmental jurisprudence, could only be nurtured by ensuring sustainable development.'[183]

In the case of *Research Foundation for Science Technology and Natural Resource Policy v. Union of India and Others*,[184] Justice S. H. Kapadia, writing for himself and for Justice Arijit Pasayat while reiterating the principle of proportionality based on the concept of balance to be applied for sustainable development, held the following: 'India after globalization is an emergent economy along with Brazil, Russia and China. India has economic growth of above 9%. However, that growth is lop-sided. A large section of the population lives below poverty line. India has largest number of youth in the world. Unemployment is endemic. Article 21/14 is the heart of the Chapter of fundamental rights. Equality of opportunity is the basic theme of Article 14. In an emergent economy, the principle of proportionality based on the concept of balance is important. It provides level playing field to different stakeholders. Ship breaking is an industry. When we apply the principle of sustainable development, we need to keep in mind the concept of development on one hand and the concepts like generation of revenue, employment and public interest on the other hand. This is where the principle of proportionality comes in.'[185]

---

[181] Ibid.

[182] 2006 (3) SCC 229.

[183] Ibid.

[184] 2007 (15) SCC 193.

[185] *Ibid.*

**Figure 9. Roman Law Sustainability Doctrine
Incorporated by the Supreme Court of India**

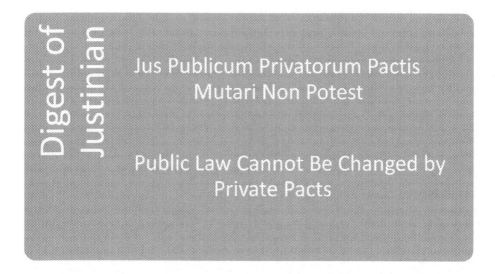

In *Reliance Natural Resources Limited v. Reliance Industries Limited*,[186] judgement was delivered by the full bench, with the Hon'ble Supreme Court consisting of Justice K. G. Balakrishnan, Justice P. Sathasivam, Justice B. S. Reddy. In the matter, Justice B. S. Reddy, writing part of the judgement, held, "'Jus publicum privatorum pactis mutari non potest." Public law cannot be changed by private pacts. Digest of Justinian. "Political democracy cannot last unless there is at its base social democracy . . . On the social plane, we have in India a society based on the principle of graded inequality, which means elevation of some and degradation of others. On the economic plane, we have a society in which there are some who have immense wealth as against many who live in abject poverty . . . How long shall we continue to live this life of contradictions? How long shall we continue to deny equality in our social and economic life? If we continue to deny it for long, we will do so only by putting our political democracy in peril. We must remove this contradiction at the earliest possible moment or else those who suffer

---

[186]   2010 (7) SCC 1.

from inequality will blow up the structure of political democracy which this Assembly has so laboriously built up".[187]

Thus, the court categorically indicated that without equality in society, no type of political superstructure is sustainable. And for sustainable development of society, social development must run parallel with all other kinds of development the society. And emphasising on maintaining intergenerational equity in the development process, the court further held, 'The concept of equality, a necessary condition for achievement of justice, is inherent in the concept of national development that we have adopted as a nation. India was never meant to be a mere land in which the desires and the Actions of the rich and the mighty take precedence over the needs of the people. The ambit and sweep of our egalitarian ideal inheres within itself the necessity of inter-generational equity. Our constitutional jurisprudence recognizes this and makes sustainable development and protection of the environment a pre-condition for the use of nature. The concept of people as a nation does not include just the living; it includes those who are unborn and waiting to be instantiated. Conservation of resources, especially scarce ones, is both a matter of efficient use to alleviate the suffering of the living and also of ensuring that such use does not lead to diminishment of the prospects of their use by future generations.'[188]

In *State of Uttaranchal v. Balwant Singh Chaufal and Others*,[189] Justice Dalveer Bhandari, writing for himself and for Justice (Dr.) Mukundakam Sharma, emphasised that the directions of the court should meet the requirements of public interest, environmental protection, elimination of pollution, and sustainable development. While ensuring sustainable development, it must be kept in view that there is no danger to the environment or ecology. The court further reiterated the principles related to sustainable development laid down in *Karnataka Industrial Areas Development Board v. Sri C. Kenchappa and Others*[190] and said that there has to be a balance between sustainable development and the environment. The court observed that before the acquisition of lands for development, the consequence and adverse impact of development on the environment must be properly

---

[187] Ibid.

[188] Ibid.

[189] AIR 2010 SC 2550.

[190] AIR 2006 SC 2038.

comprehended and the lands be acquired for development that they do not gravely impair ecology and the environment. The State Industrial Areas Development Board was tasked to incorporate the condition of allotment to obtain clearance from the Karnataka State Pollution Control Board before the land is allotted for development. The said directory condition of the allotment of lands must be converted into a mandatory condition for all the projects to be sanctioned in the future.

In the matter of *Maharashtra Land Development Corporation and Others v. State of Maharashtra and Another,*[191] Justice (Dr.) Mukundakam Sharma, writing for himself and Justice Anil R. Dave, emphasised on maintaining the fine balance between development needs and their impact on the environment and ecology. The hon'ble court held the following: 'Since Independence, India has travelled a long way on the path of progress and industrialization to achieve a better quality of life. A developing country like ours cannot afford to ignore the growing needs of teeming millions, but this development shall have to resonate with the preservation of the environment. Mahatma Gandhi once said that earth provides enough to satisfy every man's need but not every man's greed. It is the greed of the mankind which has brought environment degradation and pollution. Preservation of the eco-system is an immutable duty under the Constitution—a fine balance must be struck between environmental protection and development. Many regions in India are biodiversity "hotspots", known to host a staggering variety of flora and fauna. However, they are under the constant threat of environmental degradation and rapid depletion of natural resources, due to various factors, including the desire to earn quick money. Consequently, a major challenge in this backdrop is to arrive at a successful model of sustainable development— one that aims to preserve the rich ecosystem, while addressing the economic needs of the people in the region.'[192]

In the cases of *Lafarge Uranium Mining Private Limited* and *T. N. Godavarman Thirumulpad v. Union of India and Others,*[193] Justice S. H. Kapadia, writing for himself, Justice Aftab Alam, and Justice K. S. Radhakrishnan, held that the judicial review for scrutinising the intent of various administrative authorities is essential. Courts have to keep checking

---

[191] 86. Civil Appeal Nos. 2147–2148 of 2004; available at www.sci.co.in.
[192] [193] Ibid.
[193] AIR 2011 SC 2781.

environmental clearances and other similar policies and ensure that they confirm to various principles of sustainable development jurisprudence. It said, 'Universal human dependence on the use of environmental resources for the most basic needs renders it impossible to refrain from altering environment. As a result, environmental conflicts are ineradicable and environmental protection is always a matter of degree, inescapably requiring choices as to the appropriate level of environmental protection and the risks which are to be regulated. This aspect is recognized by the concept of "sustainable development".'[194]

The decision of this court in the case of *Narmada Bachao Andolan v. Union of India and Others* (2000 [10] SCC 664) equally well settled that the environment has different facets and that care of the environment is an ongoing process. 'These concepts rule out the formulation of across-the-board principle as it would depend on the facts of each case whether diversion in a given case should be permitted or not, barring 'No Go' areas (whose identification would again depend on undertaking of due diligence exercise). In such cases, the Margin of Appreciation Doctrine would apply. Making these choices necessitates decisions, not only about how risks should be regulated, how much protection is enough, and whether ends served by environmental protection could be pursued more effectively by diverting resources to other uses. Since the nature and degree of environmental risk posed by different activities varies, the implementation of environmental rights and duties require proper decision making based on informed reasons about the ends which may ultimately be pursued, as much as about the means for attaining them. Setting the standards of environmental protection involves mediating conflicting visions of what is of value in human life . . . Time has come for us to apply the constitutional "doctrine of proportionality" to the matters concerning environment as a part of the process of judicial review in contradistinction to merit review. It cannot be gainsaid that utilization of the environment and its natural resources has to be in a way that is consistent with principles of sustainable development and intergenerational equity, but balancing of these equities may entail policy choices. In the circumstances, barring exceptions, decisions relating to utilization of natural resources

---

[194] Ibid.

have to be tested on the anvil of the well-recognized principles of judicial review.'[195]

Declaring the natural resources of the country as public goods and the equitable distribution of these public goods a solemn duty of the state while deciding the matter between *Centre for Public Interest Litigation and Others v. Union of India and Others*,[196] Justice G. S. Singhvi, writing for himself and Justice Asok Kumar Ganguly in a very seminal case for the Indian jurisprudence, held, 'As natural resources are public goods, the doctrine of equality, which emerges from the concepts of justice and fairness, must guide the State in determining the actual mechanism for distribution of natural resources.'[197]

Figure 10. Natural Resources Declared as Public Goods by the Supreme Court of India

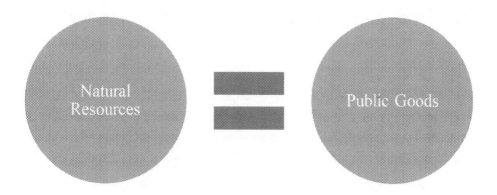

In this regard, the doctrine of equality has two aspects: First, it regulates the rights and obligations of the state vis-à-vis its people and demands that the people be granted equitable access to natural resources and/or its products and that they are adequately compensated for the transfer of the resource to the private domain. Second, it regulates the rights and obligations of the state vis-à-vis private parties seeking to acquire/use the resource and demands that the procedure adopted for distribution is just, nonarbitrary, and

---

[195] Ibid.

[196] 2012 (3) SCC 1.

[197] Ibid.

transparent and that it does not discriminate between similarly placed private parties.[198]

Indian constitutional courts have taken the matter of the violation of the right to life with utmost seriousness. Showing a great concern for homeless people, who are compelled to sleep on street pavements due to lack of housing facilities, the court directed all the Indian states to make night shelters for homeless people. A division bench of the court comprising Hon'ble Justice Dalveer Bhandari and Hon'ble Justice Dipak Mishra, while passing such orders on 23 January 2012 in IA nos. 94 and 96 in writ petition (civil) no. 196 of 2001 *People's Union for Civil Liberties v. Union of India and Others,*[199] held the following: 'Nothing is more important for the State than to preserve and protect the lives of the most vulnerable, weak, poor and helpless people. The homeless people are constantly exposed to the risk of life while living on the pavements and the streets and the threat to life is particularly imminent in the severe and biting cold winter, especially in the northern India. The State must discharge its core obligation to comply with Article 21 of the Constitution by providing night shelters for the vulnerable and homeless people.' [200]

In Re: Special Reference No. 1 of 2012,[201] which was decided on 27 September 2012, the Hon'ble Apex Court held that in a maturing society, individual rights and collective rights have to be balanced. The true effect of article 14 is to ensure that a few individuals do not enrich themselves at the cost of all others, which would amount to deprivation to the plurality (i.e. the nation itself).[202]

Judicial Response with Special Reference to Hydropower Projects in the State of Uttarakhand

With the creation of various large and small river water dams in the state of Uttarakhand, sustainability concerns also emerged. River Ganga is

---

[198] Ibid.
[199] Supreme Court of India, Record of Proceedings; available at http://www.sci.nic.in/, last visited on 9 October 2012.
[200] Ibid.
[201] 2012 (10) SCC 1.
[202] Ibid.

also considered very sacred by a large portion of India's majority Hindu population. After the creation of the separate state of Uttarakhand, majority of old hydropower projects gained momentum. The government of Uttarakhand, as part of it policy to be an energy-surplus state, also encouraged many small hydropower projects on the River Ganga or on its various tributaries. Government public sector undertakings (PSUs) like National Thermal Power Corporation (NTPC) and UJVNL (Uttarakhand Jal Vidyut Nigam Ltd.), as well as private players like GVK Shrinagar Hydro Electric Project, adopted a very aggressive approach towards the construction of hydropower projects and their commissioning. Parallel to construction of hydropower dams, a mass movement of local people also started. A large fraction of people of the hill state protested against the haphazard construction activities in the hills. A legal battle for the sustainability for the power projects in the state also reached its constitutional courts. One spirited public person, Mr. Bharat Jhunjhunwala, filed a public interest petition in the Hon'ble High Court of Uttarakhand at Nainital as *Bharat Jhunjhunwala v. Managing Director, National Hydroelectric Power Corporation and Others*[203] against the construction of Kotlibhel Stage I(A) on Bhagirathi River, Kotlibhel Stage I(B) on Alaknanda River, and Kotlibhel Stage II at Kaudiyala River. The petitioner prayed for the stoppage of construction work on these projects and also for the redesigning of their structures.[204] Another public interest petition was filed by a NGO, the Indian Council for Enviro-Legal Action, as *Indian Council for Enviro-Legal Action (ICELA) v. Union of India and Others*[205] for the stopping of blasting and construction of tunnels and dams between Gangotri and Dharasu (Uttarkashi) Hydropower projects being built by the NTPC and Uttarakhand Jal Vidut Nigam Ltd. for the state of Uttarakhand.

It was remarkable that at the same time another fraction of people in the state were very much pro–hydroelectric power, and they wanted run-of-the-river projects to be continued. Rural Litigation and Entitlement Kendra (RLEK), an NGO working in the state for the betterment of the hill and its people in the State, also filed a public interest petition in the High Court of Uttarakhand as *Rural Litigation and Entitlement Kendra (RLEK) v. State of*

---

[203]   Writ Petition (PIL) No. 211 of 2008, filed in the Hon'ble High Court of Uttarakhand at Nainital.

[204]   Ibid.

[205]   Writ Petition (PIL) 468 of 2008 in the High Court of Uttarakhand at Nainital.

Uttarakhand and Others.[206] It prayed for the continuance of run-of-the-river hydropower projects, citing reasons of development of the backward regions of the state. Based on their own research, RLEK brought before the hon'ble high court some glaring facts in its petition that despite having ambition of an energy-surplus state, there are approximately 1,200 villages in the state that are out of power—a tragic reality of the energy ambition of the state. (However, it is pertinent to mention here that the Ministry of Power of the government of India in the 'Quarterly Report of Bharat Nirman: Rural Electrification',[207] as of 31 December 2012, depicts the fact that there is no unelectrified village in the state of Uttarakhand, which is not covered under the Bharat Nirman Rural Electrification Programme.) The National Thermal Power Corporation was also successful to an extent in convincing the high court that the modern technology and its new method of the run-of-the-river scheme for the construction of the hydropower projects are sustainable modes of construction and don't harm the environment and ecology of the area. Considering the facts presented by the RLEK and NTPC, the high court considered the view that not only the concern for the environment and ecology is necessary but also poverty eradication and development of the backward regions of the state is of importance, so a sustainability approach is to be adopted.[208]

A fierce legal battle between the pro-environment and pro-development groups was being contested in the constitutional courts of the state, and the matter was under thorough examination and scrutiny of the judges. Meanwhile, under mounting pressure from the various pro-environment as well as religious groups, the union government also ordered NTPC not to proceed with the construction activities of all the hydropower projects over the River Ganga, specially the Loharinag Pala Hydro Power Project. RLEK again filed a public interest petition in the High Court of Uttarakhand as *Rural Litigation and Entitlement Kendra v. Union of India*[209] in February 2009, challenging the work stoppage order of the union government in the High Court of Uttarakhand. A division bench comprising Justice P. C. Pant

---

[206] Writ Petition (PIL) 532 of 2008 in the High Court of Uttarakhand at Nainital.

[207]

[208] 1996 (5) SCC 647.

[209] *Rural Litigation and Entitlement Kendra (RLEK) v. Union of India*, WP (PIL) 15/2009 in the Hon'ble High Court of Uttarakhand at Nainital.

and Justice B. S. Verma, after considering the fact that huge costs have already been incurred by the state company and that no credible sustainability threats have been mentioned by the union government while passing the impugned order of closure of the Loharinag Pala Hydro Power Project, stayed the union government order of stopping work at the Loharinag Pala Hydro Power Project.[210] Resumption of the power project was considered a huge victory for the pro-development group in the state.

From time to time, the high court also directed the state governments concerned and the union government in taking the proper steps for the conservation of the environment and ecology and mandated the tough environment-impact assessments (EIAs) of all the hydropower projects in the region to be done. While long drawn legal battles were going on in the constitutional courts of the state between environmentalists and development activists, the union government decided to formulate a special Ganga River basin authority for a sustainability review of all river water projects on the River Ganga. The government of India constituted the National Ganga River Basin Authority (NGRBA) on 20 February 2009 under section 3(3) of the Environment (Protection) Act of 1986 and has also given Ganga the status of a national river. The NGRBA is a specialised body for the comprehensive management of the River Ganga basin, and its mandate is to ensure development requirements in a sustainable manner to ensure ecological flows in the Ganga. The constitution of the NGRBA is very comprehensive and high powered too. The organisation is chaired by the prime minister of India and has as its members the chief ministers of the states through which the Ganga flows (Uttarakhand, Uttar Pradesh, Bihar, Jharkhand, and West Bengal). The ministers of environment and forests, finance, urban development, water resources, power, science and technology and the deputy chairman of the planning commission are also members. The organisation may coopt one or more chief ministers from any of the states having major tributaries of the River Ganga. It may also coopt up to five members who are experts in the fields of river conservation, hydrology, environmental engineering, social mobilisation, and any other related field as and when the need arises. The NGRBA project is also being funded by international agencies. The World Bank is supporting the government of India in its

---

[210]   Order dated 26 February /2009 passed by the division bench of the Hon'ble High Court of Uttarakhand at Nainital in Writ Petition No. 15/2009 (PIL).

efforts to achieve this national goal. In 2011, it has committed to providing $1.556 billion for the National Ganga River basin project, with $1 billion in financing from the World Bank Group, including a $199 million interest-free IDA credit and $801 million low-interest IBRD loan, which will be implemented over eight years. The project will support the National Ganga River Basin Authority (NGRBA) in building the capacity of its nascent operational-level institutions so that they can manage the long-term Ganga clean-up and conservation programme. Apart from dedicated operational-level institutions at the central and state levels, the project will also help the NGRBA set up a state-of-the-art Ganga Knowledge Centre to act as a repository for knowledge relevant to the conservation of the Ganga.[211]

The 'maintenance of minimum ecological flows in the river Ganga with the aim of ensuring water quality and environmentally sustainable development' is one of the specific functions of the NGRBA. For the construction of hydropower projects, the building of reservoirs (like in the case of the Tehri Hydro Power Project) was the major criticism and posed environmental as well as ecological threats for the local areas involved. The NGRBA is reviewing hydropower projects on the River Ganga and its tributaries to ensure minimum ecological flows in the Ganga. Small run-of-the-river hydropower projects have become a golden solution for the long tussle between environmentalists and development activists. An early assessment of the state government and the policy framework as mentioned above for small hydropower projects shall benefit the energy requirements of the state as well as satisfy its sustainability concerns. After the constitution of the NGRBA, the High Court of Uttarakhand also sent all the pending matters before it with regard to various hydropower projects in the state of Uttarakhand for the consideration of said authority.[212]

Since then, the NGRBA is the empowered agency headed by no less than the prime minister of the country, which is taking care of the important decisions with regard to hydropower projects on the national river Ganga. However, it is pertinent to note here that the mood of the nation and its people are growing completely different from the pressure groups headed

---

[211] See http://www.worldbank.org/en/news/2011/05/27/india-the-national-ganga-river-basin-project (web link last visited on 28 November 2012).

[212] Order dated 18 May 2009 passed by Hon'ble High Court of Uttarakhand at Nainital in Writ Petition (PIL) 532 of 2008.

by seers and sages. It got reflected in a very recent observation made by the Supreme Court of India over resulting delays and cost escalations in the construction of hydropower projects while dismissing a plea challenging a hydroelectric project on the Alaknanda River in Uttarakhand. Dismissing a petition challenging the Vishnugad Pipalkoti hydroelectric project, a bench of Justices H. L. Dattu and Ranjan Gogoi said, 'The moment a power project is to start, litigation is filed in court. If initially the project cost is Rs 1,000 crore, it escalates to Rs 10,000 crore over the years and tax-payers money is wasted.'[213]

In a meeting of the NGRBA held on 17 April 2012, the chief minister of Uttarakhand specifically expressed the developmental needs of the state and (contrary to the demand of scrapping all the hydropower projects in the state raised by various self-styled religious leaders based on no scientific evidence whatsoever) emphasised that his state is committed to preserving the Ganga:

> However the development of the State is equally important and the need of the people living on the banks of the river I the higher reaches is required to be given consideration. Thus, hydro-power generation in the State in a balanced manner and on scientific basis is necessary as only a fraction of the potential has been tapped so far. He requested the following based on the decisions taken in an all-party meeting as well as the Cabinet of the State:
>
> (i) Detailed basin studies should be carried out to determine the requirement for environmental flow, which should be agreed by all and monitored regularly.
> (ii) The work on the nine hydro-electric projects should not be stopped and the work on already closed projects should be started again.
> (iii) The 135 km stretch of river Ganga from Gaumukh to Uttarkashi should not be notified as eco-sensitive zone, as it will impede the developmental activities in the region and the existing

---

[213] See *Times of India* online edition on 25 January 2013, 02.55 a.m. IST; available at http://articles.timesofindia.indiatimes.com/2013-01-25/india/36546959_1_power-projects-kudankulam-nuclear-power-plant.

environmental laws are adequate for ensuring the conservation of Ganga.

(iv) Mining of sand should not be stopped and it should be allowed to be carried out in scientific manner.

(v) All NGRBA projects in Uttarakhand should be funded on 90:10 basis.[214]

Authority as high level as chaired by the prime minister of the nation did not take any substantial decision on such a vital issue. None of the concerns raised by the chief minister of the Uttarakhand (specially after an all-party support and a cabinet decision on the issue) were addressed by the authority; a very inconclusive decision was taken at the end of the meeting that a 'multi-disciplinary group shall further be formed to look holistically at the various options available and recommend broad principles and actions that need to be taken with regard to conservation, irrigation use and running of hydro-electric projects that will ensure uninterrupted flow of the river Ganga. Based on the recommendations of the multi-disciplinary group, a road map would be drawn up for further action'.[215]

One peculiar aspect came into light during the study of court cases touching upon the issues of the construction of hydropower projects in the state of Uttarakhand. It was noted that the major litigation happened not against the government or its subsidiaries but amongst the government and its instrumentalities. During the interviews of the officers of the public sector companies involved in the hydropower generation in the state of Uttarakhand, it was felt as though they were totally disconnected from the government machinery and seemed to have no better coordination and cooperation with government agencies than other private sector companies involved in the area.

One such case was *National Thermal Power Corporation v. Union of India and Others*,[216] in which the public sector company National Thermal Power Corporation approached the hon'ble high court against the Union of

---

[214] Minutes of the third meeting of the National Ganga River Basin Authority (NGRBA) held on 17 April 2012, NGRBA, Ministry of Environment and Forest Government of India.

[215] Ibid.

[216] Writ Petition No. 2455 of 2011 in the High Court of Uttarakhand.

India through the Ministry of Environment and Forests of the government of India with the following prayer: '(i) Issue a writ, order or direction in the nature of mandamus to the respondent no 1 to decided the review petition/ representation dated 23-05-2011 of the petitioner with regard to the forest clearance for the Rupsiabagad-Khasiabada Hydro Electricity Project with in a period of one month or with in such reasonable period, which is found appropriate by this Hon'ble Court.' The high court passed following order: 'The petitioner's representation for reconsideration of diversion of 217.522 hectares of forest land for Hydro power Project is pending consideration before the competent authority since 9th September 2010. Without going into the veracity and legality of the representation so made, this petition is disposed of with a direction to the authority concerned to decide the representation of the petitioner by the reasoned and speaking order within three months from the date of the production of the certified copy of this order.'[217]

This was a situation in which the government (as NTPC is a fully owned company of the government of India) was compelled to approach the Hon'ble High Court of Uttarakhand against the very own government of India and, in particular, the Ministry of Environment and Forests just to get directions from the high court to the Ministry of Environment to decide on the forest clearance for the project.

As this was not enough, after this order, the Ministry of Environment and Forests declined to give clearance for the diversion of 217.522 hectares of forest land for the hydropower project; and ultimately, after spending a considerable amount of public funds on the project, NTPC was forced to withdraw the whole Rupsiabagad Khasiabada Hydro Electricity Project from the state of Uttarakhand. It seems to be a classic example of a lack of coordination between the government and its own corporations, leading to inordinate delays and waste of public money. It was a situation when the instrumentality of the government had to take direction from the court against the government just to make a decision. Today, the only remains from the dead Rupsiabagad Khasiabada Hydro Electricity Project is a lesson that had there been better coordination and cooperation amongst the government and its agencies, a lot of public money could have been saved, and perhaps

---

[217] Order dated 22 November 2011 passed by the Hon'ble High Court of Uttarakhand in WPMS No. 2455 of 2011.

the remote hills of the state of Uttarakhand hitherto untouched by any developmental activities would have witnessed some growth in the area.

While interviewing one of the senior law officers of the NTPC Ltd., an interesting observation was made by him: 'Most of the engineers of our company are so much busy in fighting court cases, there is hardly any engineers engaged in actual engineering work!' Too much litigation and the resulting closure of the hydropower projects after spending a substantial amount of money in field surveys as well as preliminary investments is certainly not a very healthy sign of the development of hydropower projects in the state. Apart from a series of public interest petitions filed against each and every major hydropower projects, the Hon'ble High Court of Uttarakhand, and consequential regulatory as well as correctional orders, a curious case happened between a hydropower company and the government of the state in the matter of *NTPC Ltd. v. State of Uttarakhand*.[218] In this case, NTPC Ltd. is developing Tapovan Vishnugad hydropower project on the river Dhauliganga in the district of Chamoli in the state of Uttarakhand. It had a proposed installed capacity of 520 MW, which has been allocated to the petitioner corporation by the government of Uttarakhand on a Build-Own-Operate-Maintain (BOOM) basis through an implementation agreement dated 23 June 2004.[219] In this apparently avoidable litigation, NTPC Ltd. approached the hon'ble high court for a stay against the order of the district magistrate, Chamoli, slapping a penalty of five times the value of the muck that came out as a by-product of the excavation of land for the purpose of constructing a barrage. The request of the power company to pay the actual royalty amount was curiously turned down by the district magistrate just for the sake of imposing a penalty. At a preliminary stage, after considering the case of the petitioner that neither the digging for construction of a barrage and the consequential excavation of sand can be defined as mining nor its storage on the construction site can be termed illegal in violation of the Mines and Minerals (Development and Regulation) Act of 1957. The penalty part of the order was stayed by the Hon'ble High Court of Uttarakhand (vide

---

[218] Writ Petition No. 2607 of 2011 (M/S) filed on 13 December 2011 in the Hon'ble High Court of Uttarakhand.

[219] See implementation agreement between NTPC Limited and the government of Uttaranchal for the execution of Tapovan Vishnugad 520 MW Hydro Electric Power Project in Uttaranchal dated 23 June 2004.

an interim order dated 14 December 2011).[220] (Writ petition is still pending consideration of the hon'ble high court).

However, it is pertinent to mention here that the division bench of the hon'ble high court has already settled the law in this regard in the case of *Jaiprakash Associates Limited v. State of Uttaranchal*,[221] in which the court also quashed the demand made by the district magistrate from the petitioners for the royalty of the stones, which the petitioners dug out from their own land as a by-product of digging the foundation of the building. The court held that to be mining operation under the said act, mining or digging must be done with the intention of winning the mineral from the land.

The very nature of prayers and orders passed by the respective courts in the above-mentioned court cases show that these litigations are completely avoidable for a hydropower company if not so unnecessary, specially against the very government for which it is implementing the project. Such litigation and the utter lack of coordination with the state machinery certainly results in undue delays in the implementation of projects and also give rise to project costs.

Response of the Supreme Court of India to the Severe Destruction in Uttarakhand Due to Flood and Erosion during 16–17 June 2013

In the state of Uttarakhand, excessive rainfall and weather conditions happened during the middle of June 2013. A monumental tragedy happened in the state. A large number of people living alongside the river and in the hilly regions witnessed nature in its very cruel state, and a large number of people were left homeless and displaced. The approximate number of villages affected were 1,603, with 108,653 people directly affected and 4,726 houses fully damaged.[222]

---

[220] Interim order dated 14 December 2011 passed in Writ Petition No. 2607 of 2011 (M/S) *NTPC Ltd. V. State of Uttarakhand*.

[221] AIR 2007 (Utt) 41.

[222] 'Repair, Renovation, and Restoration of Water Bodies', Standing Committee on Water Resources' (2013–2014), Fifteenth Lok Sabha, Ministry of Water Resources, Review of Ganga Flood Control Commission; available at http://164.100.47.134/lsscommittee/Water% 20Resources/15_Water_Resources_21.pdf.

The scale of the tragedy was such that the government of the state was compelled to ask for help, even from international agencies like the World Bank and the Asian Development Bank despite a lot of support provided by the government of India. As the aftermath to the unprecedented tragedy, various groups were formed, and the government tried to ascertain the causes of nature's fury as well as preventive measures, if any. Keeping in view of the situation, the Ministry of Water Resources (MoWR) constituted the Ganga Flood Control Commission to find the causes of the severe destruction in Uttarakhand due to flood and erosion during 16–17 June 2013. This committee submitted its detailed report to the government with the reasons for such a mass disaster caused by severe weather conditions and also suggested preventive measures.[223]

Flood moderation by the Tehri reservoir found special mention in the report of the committee: '5.1.5 Flood Moderation by Tehri Reservoir: It was observed that the water level along river Mandakini, on river Alaknanda from Rudraprayag to Devprayag and along Ganga downstream of Devprayag had either surpassed the previous HFL or were very near to the same. The situation started getting milder downstream of Devprayag. One of the possible reasons for this could be the flood moderation by the Tehri Reservoir. The situation was analyzed on the basis of water level and discharge observations at various places in the region. It was observed that maximum discharge observed at Haridwar at Bhimgoda Barrage was about 5.25 Lakh cusecs at 19:00 Hrs on 17.06.2013. The same gradually fell down to about 2.65 Lakh cusec at 23:00 Hrs on 18.06.2013. The maximum inflow to the Tehri Reservoir during the above period was 2.65 Lakh cusec at 04:00 Hrs on 17.06.2013 while outflow from Tehri Dam at that time was only about 0.13 Lakh cusecs. As such, in absence of Tehri reservoir, the flow which was absorbed in the reservoir could have impinged on reaches downstream of Devprayag. Keeping in view, the travel time of flood in river Bhagirathi/Ganga from Tehri to Haridwar (as per records of CWC) being about 09.00 Hrs. The absorbed flow of about 2.52 Lakh Cusecs might also have reached Haridwar by 13:00 Hrs of 17.06.2013. The detail analysis of the hydrograph indicates that the flow at Bhimgoda barrage would have been more than 6.5 Lakhs cusecs in that case. In view of above, it is evident that existence

---

[223] Committee constituted (vide Order No. 1/15/2013-IEC/587-607), Government of India, Ministry of Water Resources, 2014.

of a storage structure definitely moderated the flood condition. It can also be concluded that the reservoir can be operated so as to provide flood benefit even the same has not been constructed for providing flood benefit exclusively. In view of above, it is suggested that action for construction of large storages, wherever feasible, on Alaknanda/Mandakini/Pindar headstream of the Ganga river system may be taken at the earliest. These storages could be operated in a manner to provide opportunity for absorption of flood in unfavorable condition.' [224]

One of the conclusions reached by the above-mentioned committee is very crucial for this research, and that is clearly in favour of the construction of large dams like the Tehri Dam in the state of Uttarakhand. The conclusion above and consequent recommendation is quoted as follows: 'It is evident that the existence of large storage in Tehri Dam was helpful in absorbing a substantial amount of flow in Bhagirathi River. The flood situation in the reach downstream of Devprayag could have been further worse in absence of Tehri Dam. The highest observed discharge in river Ganga at Haridwar was about 5.25 cusec during the current episode. This could have been more than 6.5 lakh cusecs in the absence of Tehri Dam.'[225] Further, the committee recommended that 'construction of large storages, wherever feasible, on Alaknanda/Mandakini/Pindar headstream of the Ganga river system. These storages could be operated in a manner to provide opportunity for absorption of flood in unfavourable condition. Possibility of storage on tributaries may also be explored'.[226]

The above-mentioned conclusions and consequential recommendations in the report of the committee constituted by the Ministry of Water Resources to find the causes of the severe destruction in Uttarakhand due to flooding and erosion during 16–17 June 2013 clearly demonstrate the utility of large reservoirs and big dams in this hilly state. Recent voices of concern from all parts of society as high as from the Supreme Court of India must consider this positive aspect of big dams before deciding on the issue of hydropower projects in the state. A division bench of the Hon'ble Supreme Court of India consisting of Justice K. S. Radhakrishnan and Justice Dipak Misra expressed its concern on the tragedy in June 2013 in the state of Uttarakhand

---

[224] Id. at p. 49.

[225] Ibid. See p. 63.

[226] Ibid. See p. 64.

in the case of *Alaknanda Hydro Power Co. Ltd. v. Anuj Joshi and Others*[227] in the following words: 'We are, however, very much concerned with the mushrooming of large number of hydroelectric projects in the State of Uttarakhand and its impact on Alaknanda and Bhagirathi river basins.'[228]

The hon'ble court, amongst many, passed one very crucial direction for any future construction and sanctioning of hydropower projects in the state: 'We direct the MoEF as well as State of Uttarakhand not to grant any further environmental clearance or forest clearance for any hydroelectric power project in the State of Uttarakhand, until further orders.'[229]

The 'report of the Committee constituted by Ministry of Water Resources to find the causes for severe destruction in Uttarakhand due to flood and erosion during 16–17 June 2013'[230] did not find any mention in the hon'ble apex judgement, while the hon'ble court relied on various other committees and reports much earlier in time than the June 2013 tragedy. Finally, the same judgement also directed government agencies to do more concrete research work on the causes and effects of such natural disasters in the state of Uttarakhand and also to find out if there are any linkages between the construction of man-made hydropower projects and natural disasters.

In October 2013, the Ministry of Environment and Forests constituted an expert body (EB), as directed by the supreme court, 'to make a detailed study as to whether Hydroelectric Power Projects existing and under construction have contributed to the environmental degradation, if so, to what extent and also whether it has contributed to the present tragedy occurred at Uttarakhand in the month of June 2013' and with a few other related directions. Unfortunately, before any other outcome, some serious differences arose amongst the EB itself, and the Central Water Commission (CWC) and Central Electricity Authority (CEA) disassociated themselves from the rest of the EB and decided to prepare a separate report on the issue. Two serious flaws were pointed out by the CWC and CEA members in the formation of the EB. One of them was that the Uttarakhand state should have been represented by the power department, which is responsible for the

---

[227] Civil Appeal No. 6736 of 2013, judgment dated August 13, 2013; available at www.sci.nic.in.

[228] Ibid. See p. 62.

[229] Ibid. See p. 70.

[230] 2001 (2) SCC 62.

development of hydroelectric projects in Uttarakhand instead of the irrigation department. Another problem was that there has been no representation from an organisation dealing with meteorology like the India Meteorology Department, which has a major role to play in the EB. CWC and CEA cited their objection in their separate report as follows: 'As per the directions of the Hon'ble Supreme Court and the orders issued by the MoEF, CWC and CEA have been attending various meetings of the EB from the start of the proceedings. CWC and CEA representatives had patiently and sincerely attended all the deliberations including the field visits from the beginning to the end except the last meeting held at Dehradun for wrapping up the report. During these participations, quality inputs based on realistic data were presented to help EB to complete its task. However, after observing the casual attitude of the members from the NGO sides and withdrawal and non-representation from many institutions, it was apparent that the EB will provide a report based on its biased perceptions and devoid of any real expert opinions. CWC and CEA were of the view that by becoming signatory to such report, they will be acting against the stated policies of Government of India and the techno-economic issues involved in this matter. In view of these important consideration, CWC and CEA have informed to EB on 5.3.2014 about their stand of disassociation with the EB. Notwithstanding above, it is expected from EB that it will take on record the contribution of CWC and CEA.'[231]

Despite the above-mentioned differences, the EB decided to proceed further; hence, two separate reports came out one from the CWC and CEA and another from the rest of the EB, which were submitted to the Hon'ble Supreme Court of India. Because of the two conflicting reports, the Ministry of Environment and Forests sought further time from the Hon'ble Supreme Court of India to constitute yet another expert committee on the issue, and the court passed the following order: 'We have gone through both the Reports. We feel that it would be appropriate to give an opportunity to the MoEF to examine the Reports and come out with concrete reasons for constituting another Committee. We have gone through both the Reports. We feel that it would be appropriate to give an opportunity to the MoEF to

---

[231] See Report of CWC and CEA on Uttarakhand Disaster and Hydropower Projects (Expert Body constituted by MoEF under the Directions of the Hon'ble Supreme Court of India), p. 5.

examine the Reports and come out with concrete reasons for constituting another Committee.'[232]

Implementation Mechanisms by the Courts

For quite a long time, it kept us agitated against judicial orders having executive tone and tenors. It was always a cause for concern that the judiciary in India was overreaching its brief. But now after having a look on the repeated failures of the executive limb of the government and there being an advent of judicial orders having a certain 'implementation structure' within themselves and a complete consonance of the executive for this kind of system, in no uncertain terms, I believe that such a judicial governance is a reality of the day and definitely, as far as the present political setup remains unchanged, irreversible too.

Classically, though, judgements once delivered were left for the executive to implement (except contempt jurisdiction, where courts can force for the compliance of orders). Now it is imperative on judges to provide not only ratio/ obiter in any case of social and public importance but also an implementation mechanism in itself. For example, in the case of *Samaj Parivartan Samudaya v. State of Karnataka,*[233] the Hon'ble Supreme Court not only provided the idea of sustainable development to be developed further by way of creation of a 'special purpose vehicle' out of 10 per cent of the sale proceeds of the ore sold by e-auction.

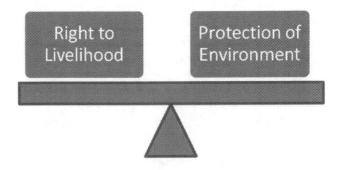

---

[232] Order dated 7 May 2014 in *Alaknanda Hydro Power Co. Ltd. v. Anuj Joshi and Others*, Civil Appeal No. 6736 of 2013; full text available at www.sci.nic.in.

[233] 2013 (8) SCC 154.

In the matter of *Goa Foundation v. Union of India*,[234] while balancing the 'right to livelihood' of 1.5 Lakh people directly employed in mining and jobs connected with mining in Goa, with the 'protection of environment', the hon'ble supreme court—in exercising its powers under article 32 and further recognising such balance as a necessary component of sustainable development—directed for 10 per cent of the sale proceeds of iron ore excavated in the state of Goa and sold by the lessees must be appropriated towards the Goa Iron Ore Permanent Fund for the purpose of sustainable development and intergenerational equity.

In both the above-mentioned matters, the hon'ble apex court took the route of monitoring committees created by its own judicial orders for the purpose ordinarily fulfilled through regular executive agencies of the state. Clearly, the court could not trust any of the existing executive agencies for the assessment and correction of the very idea of creating a special purpose vehicle.

Sustainable Development and the U.S, Supreme Court

A comparative analysis is a must to understand the level of concern and care shown by the Supreme Court of India. A comparison with the Supreme Court of the United States is imperative, as the U.S. Supreme Court is 'first amongst the equals' choice when it comes to comparing countries with their sustainability concerns, it being the biggest consumer of world energy resources, be it fossil fuels, nuclear, hydro, etc.

The role of the Supreme Court of the United States has not been so active in comparison with the Indian Supreme Court. 'None of the environmental cases decided thus far during the tenure of Chief Justice Roberts engage sustainability. The word "sustainability" does not appear to exist before the Court. It does not appear in any majority, concurring, or dissenting opinion. While the Court seems to be agnostic about the idea of sustainability as a governing norm.'[235] Sustainability concerns have not found even a single mention in the entirety of Roberts's court. Even related concerns regarding biodiversity, land use, air pollutant emissions, and clean-up standards could

---

[234]   2014 (6) SCC 590.

[235]   James R. May, 'Not at All: Environmental Sustainability in the Supreme Court', *Sustainable Development Law & Policy*, Fall 2009, pp. 20–29, 81–82.

not impress upon the court; and in majority of cases, these concerns could not implicate sustainable development ideas in the court decisions.

In *Winter v. Natural Resources Defense Council (NRDC)*,[236] the court reversed the U.S. Court of Appeals for the Ninth Circuit and ruled that the U.S. Navy's interests in security and military preparedness outweigh the respondent's interest in protecting whales and other marine mammals from acoustic harm caused by a submarine seeking sonar devices.[237]

In *Burlington Northern v. United States*,[238] the court reversed the Ninth Circuit and held 8–1 that liability as an 'arranger' under the Comprehensive Environmental Response Compensation and Liability Act (CERCLA) requires more than knowledge of chemical spillage; one must intend or plan to arrange for the disposal at issue.[239] This judgement is in clear contravention of the principles of strict liability (being followed and provided by the Supreme Court in India and the courts of many other developing countries imbibing sustainable development principles in their respective jurisdictions). Such an exemption from strict liability is not an indication of a judicial system that is environment-friendly or gives primacy to sustainable development concerns over any other thing. Justice Stevens concluded, 'Shell was not liable as an arranger under CERCLA because it did not "intend' for its chemicals to be released into the environment, even though it knew it was delivering its product to a sloppy operator.'[240] Strict liability principles, being one of the fundamental principles in sustainable development jurisprudence, would not allow such exemption of an agency who was the originator of the hazardous substance just because it didn't intend for its chemicals to be released into the environment even though it knew it was delivering its product to a sloppy operator. Troubled by the 'blind eye arrangers', Justice Ginsburg, however, ruled in favour of sustainability concerns: 'Justice Ginsburg urged a position more consistent with sustainability. She argued in dissent that Shell had arranged for disposal because it exercised "the control rein" over delivery of the D-D pesticide, specifying transportation and storage features

---

[236]   *Winter v. Natural Res. Def. Council*, 129 S. Ct. 365 (2008).

[237]   Ibid.

[238]   *BNSF Ry. Co. v. United States*, 129 S. Ct. 1870 (2009).

[239]   Ibid.

[240]   Id. at 1878–1879.

that resulted in "inevitable" spills and leaks.'[241] Holding the strict liability principles in her dissenting judgement, she held that 'the sales of useful substances [doesn't] exonerate Shell from liability, for the sales necessarily and immediately resulted in the leakage of hazardous substances'.[242]

A brief analysis of the above-mentioned cases makes it apparent that sustainable development ideas have not been incorporated into jurisprudence by the Supreme Court of the United States, neither directly nor indirectly. One specific reason is that the United States itself lacks any substantive sustainable development legislation. A country having legislations like the Alien Torts Claims Act that could not legislate any sustainable development law for itself is surprising, more so when it preaches about sustainability concerns to the whole developing world. It establishes that aside from the legislative initiatives, not even the courts in the United States, 'the biggest consumer and the polluter of the world resources', have been forthcoming in addressing sustainability concerns. Apart from some pollution-related matters, sustainable development has been out of the legislative and judicial domains of the United States. 'Early returns suggest that environmental cases hold interest for the Roberts Court. It already has decided about a dozen core environmental cases in three years, almost three times the rate during the Burger and Rehnquist Courts. Yet, sustainability seems to matter not at all.'[243]

---

[241] Id. at 1885 (Ginsberg, J., dissenting).

[242] Id.

[243] Supra note 106 at p. 29.

CHAPTER VI

SUSTAINABLE DEVELOPMENT CASE STUDY OF THE HYDROPOWER PROJECTS IN THE STATE OF UTTARAKHAND

Empirical Observations

Law is organic, and it is nurtured by the people and their opinions. The area of the present empirical study is the whole state of Uttarakhand in general and the areas having hydropower projects in particular. Since then, the inception of the generation of hydropower has been considered a major developmental activity in the state, and the state of Uttarakhand has made policies for the construction of large dams like the Tehri Dam or micro hydro projects (MHPs). There are hydropower projects on almost all the major river systems of the state. These hydro projects, either in the form of large dams or micro hydro projects or run-of-the-river projects, affect the lives of a large number of people in the state. Thus, it was felt necessary to gather the public opinion on the subject.

The study raised various socio-legal aspects and attempted to find out the level of awareness amongst the residents of Uttarakhand about the impact of hydropower projects in their lives and surroundings. It also attempted to find out whether there was any adverse impact on the environment and the people of the state due to the presence of a large number of hydropower projects in the state: What is the role of these power projects in the local area of development? What role can the courts play in the regulation of the construction of hydropower projects in the state?

The spatial or universal for the present case study was Garhwal and Kumaon regions of the state of Uttarakhand. The study was conducted in all thirteen districts of the state with more focus on the Garhwal region, and 150 respondents were selected in thirteen districts on the basis of random sampling. Tools adopted for investigation were specifically prepared questionnaires and, in some cases, interviews conducted with the help of the questionnaire. Standard statistical tools were used to analyze data, and following, charts were prepared.

The main findings of the study are as follows:

Sustainability and Hydropower Projects

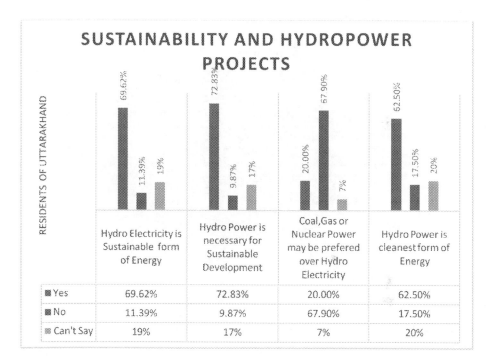

RESIDENTS OF UTTARAKHAND	Hydro Electricity is Sustainable form of Energy	Hydro Power is necessary for Sustainable Development	Coal,Gas or Nuclear Power may be prefered over Hydro Electricity	Hydro Power is cleanest form of Energy
■ Yes	69.62%	72.83%	20.00%	62.50%
■ No	11.39%	9.87%	67.90%	17.50%
▓ Can't Say	19%	17%	7%	20%

Figure 1

A large number of people definitely support the idea of hydropower being the most sustainable way of energy production, and they also consider it necessary for sustainable development in the state. While voting positively for hydropower as being the cleanest form of energy, any preference in favour of coal, gas, or nuclear power has been categorically denied by majority of voters. Contrary to the fact that usable coal and gas are already either in short supply or are difficult to supply, hydropower is as perennial as the river water itself and seems to be a sustainable way of energy production.

Balancing Ecological Protection with the Development
of Hydropower Projects in the State

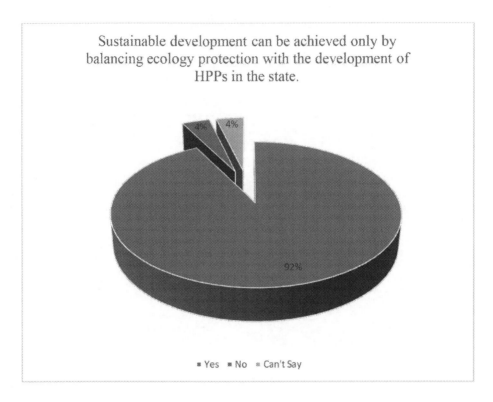

Sustainable development can be achieved only by balancing ecology protection with the development of HPPs in the state.

4% 4%

92%

▪ Yes ▪ No ▪ Can't Say

Figure 2

As many as 92 per cent of the respondents interviewed were of the opinion that sustainable development can be achieved only by balancing ecological protection with the development of hydropower projects in the state. The companies establishing hydropower projects need to work towards balancing ecological protection with sustainable development. There is a need to mitigate and compensate for the environmental impacts of hydropower projects and restore a balanced ecosystem. The need for development and protection of the environment both are important. A strategy to balance both is required to address the growing needs of humanity and to ensure sustainable development.

Alienation of Hydropower

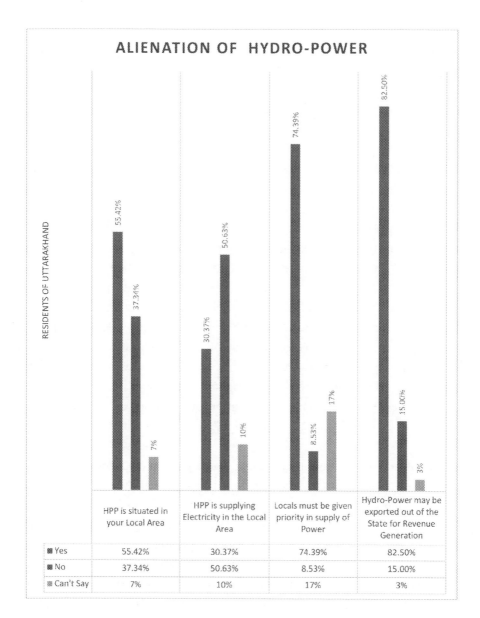

Figure 3

The alienation of hydropower is a major contentious area for the local people of Uttarakhand. After being produced in the hydropower projects running in the state of Uttarakhand, electricity is being supplied to areas outside the state. The right of first use is being denied to the people of the state in almost all major hydropower projects. In majority of the river systems in the state, either the state government or the central government has planned hydropower projects. As per the survey from different parts of the state, almost more than half of the population live in areas where hydropower projects exist in near vicinity. Apart from some very small or micro hydro projects, almost all major hydro projects in the state are built with the primary object of exporting electricity.

The primary reason quoted for this unequal power sharing is the large capital invested by agencies outside the state. It is understandable that capital is the primary requirement for the construction and operation of any hydropower project, but at the same time, it must be borne in mind that the local people of the state bear the brunt of nature if something goes not as per design. The mere investment of capital should not allow people from outside the state to take away majority of the share of electricity production. The local populace must be the prime beneficiary of such hydropower projects. However, a thumping majority of the residents of the state feel that the electricity generated within the state may be exported for revenue generation. But an almost equal majority feel that the local people must be given priority in the supply of the indigenously generated electricity.

This phenomenon is named 'alienation of hydropower,' taking analogy from the doctrine of alienation propounded by Karl Marx with regard to labour in a capital market. The theory was that labour belongs to the proletariat and often remains alienated from the use and enjoyment of the very outcome or product of labour that it produces. Likewise, in the state of Uttarakhand, the people remain deprived from the very power they participate in the production, as it is often supplied outside the state. The mere reason of investment does not give the people outside of the state the right to have first use over the electricity being produced. The people of the state have every right to claim first use of the electricity being generated in the state primarily at the cost of their ecology and environment.

Impact of Hydropower Projects (HPPs) on the Ecosystem of the State

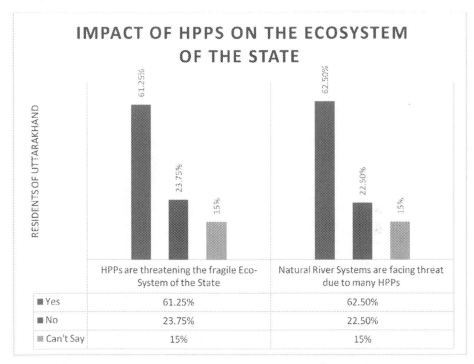

	HPPs are threatening the fragile Eco-System of the State	Natural River Systems are facing threat due to many HPPs
■ Yes	61.25%	62.50%
■ No	23.75%	22.50%
▓ Can't Say	15%	15%

Figure 4

The massive natural calamity of June 2013 in Uttarakhand has raised various questions about the link between the construction of hydropower projects and natural calamities. The increasing pressure on natural resources has often resulted in threats to the fragile ecosystems. When asked if the hydropower projects were threatening the fragile ecosystem of the state, 61 per cent of the respondents replied in the affirmative, while 62 per cent stated that natural river systems are facing threats due to many hydropower projects. It goes on to show that the haphazard construction of substandard projects cannot be a solution to the energy needs of the state. The residents of the state are equally sensitive about its fragile ecosystem and also have a high regard for the natural river systems in the state. Apart from the demand of maintaining the minimum flow in the rivers, it is imperative on the part of the hydropower companies to have a sustainable view of utilisation of the natural resources of the state. Mere profit motives cannot guide hydropower companies.

Local Area Development Due to Hydropower Projects (HPPs)

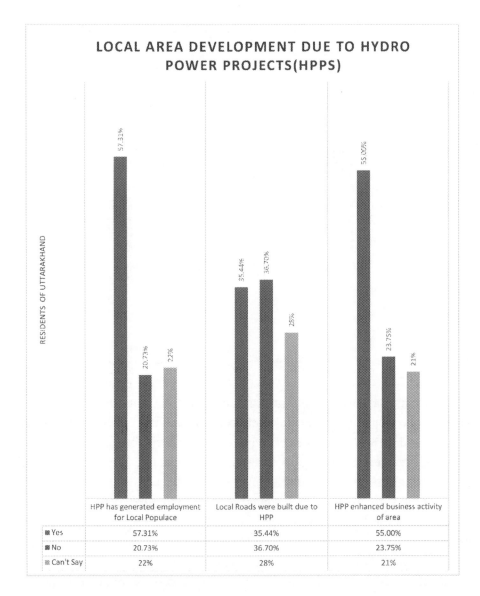

LOCAL AREA DEVELOPMENT DUE TO HYDRO POWER PROJECTS(HPPS)		
	HPP has generated employment for Local Populace	Local Roads were built due to HPP	HPP enhanced business activity of area
Yes	57.31%	35.44%	55.00%
No	20.73%	36.70%	23.75%
Can't Say	22%	28%	21%

Figure 5

A major argument in favour of the existence of hydropower projects in the state is local area development, which is in regard to employment generation in the state. Technology transfer and the improvement of social

174

conditions of the residents of the state are also the side effects that people look forward to apart from mere electricity generation. Hydropower projects bring not only economic prosperity to the state but also social stability in the local area. In the past, a large-scale migration of people from the hills was one of the state's problems. The presence of hydropower projects in the remote hill areas has also checked off this peculiar problem of the hills. With a future investment in the remote areas, people tend to stay back and participate in various economic opportunities and social activities generated due to the hydropower projects in the remote parts of the hills in the state. In regard to employment generation due to the establishment of hydropower projects, majority of the respondents have replied in the affirmative that the hydropower projects have generated employment opportunities to local communities. This goes to prove that hydropower projects have the added advantage of providing income-generation avenues for the local people. A mere 20 per cent of the respondents replied in the negative that these projects do not provide employment to local communities. Time and again, the need for hydropower projects vis-à-vis employment has also been favourably argued. This lends economic vitality to not just the local people but also the economy. In regard to hydropower projects and development (in this case, the construction of roads), there has been no majority view provided by the respondents, making it clear that the development of roads has not been given priority by companies setting up hydropower projects. Therefore, affirmative action needs to be taken in regard to the construction of roads, especially in a state like Uttarakhand, where many villages are not connected to the roadhead, and the harsh topography and climatic conditions make accessibility the need of the hour. On being asked if hydropower projects enhanced business activities of the area, majority replied in the positive. This further reinforces the fact that hydropower projects positively impact economies where they are established. The bearing of hydropower projects on the economy cannot be ignored, and they provide employment opportunities to the people; what needs to be looked at is the development/ construction of roads where these projects are established, which will lend more impetus to development in the region in particular and in the nation as a whole.

The Influence of Hydropower Projects (HPPs) on Local Ecology

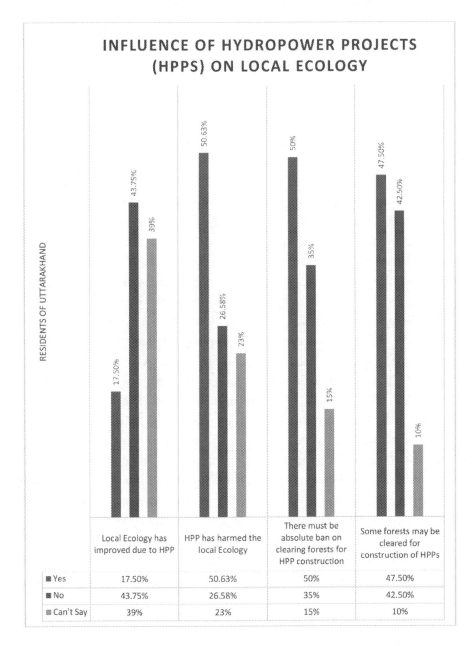

INFLUENCE OF HYDROPOWER PROJECTS (HPPS) ON LOCAL ECOLOGY

RESIDENTS OF UTTARAKHAND

	Local Ecology has improved due to HPP	HPP has harmed the local Ecology	There must be absolute ban on clearing forests for HPP construction	Some forests may be cleared for construction of HPPs
Yes	17.50%	50.63%	50%	47.50%
No	43.75%	26.58%	35%	42.50%
Can't Say	39%	23%	15%	10%

Figure 6

There has been a growing debate on the effect of hydropower projects on ecology. It has been argued by some proponents that there needs to be a balance between development and nature, and both cannot be taken for granted; in fact, they should complement and supplement each other. On being questioned if local ecology has improved due to hydropower projects, a minority of the respondents interviewed replied in the affirmative, whereas a large portion replied in the negative; 39 per cent, however, did not have an answer to the same. This brings to light the fact that ecology needs to be looked into when such projects are set up and post their operation, and environmental gradation/protection should be given impetus. On the issue of harm caused by hydropower projects to the local ecology majority were of the view that it has had a negative impact on local ecology. This emphasises the need to reconcile the conflict between development and ecological conversation in the larger interest of the country. There must be an absolute ban on the clearing of forests; hydropower project construction was supported by majority of the respondents interviewed, whereas 30 per cent of them did not agree to the same. In this backdrop, it needs to be stated that people believe that development and the environment need to go together, and for the setting up of hydropower projects, deforestation needs to be put to an end.

On being asked if some forests may be cleared for the construction of hydropower projects, almost the same percentage of people replied in the affirmative and negative, thereby giving the view that development is required but needs to be seen through a sustainable development perspective; and where possible, a negotiation needs to be met between the two. An interesting fact that has come out of the above-mentioned survey is that more than 50 per cent of the residents have confirmed the harm being done by the presence of hydropower projects on the local ecology. It may include the flora and fauna of the area as well as the lifestyle of the people and the ecologically fragile lands in the area. Local people have given a mixed response on the cutting of trees for the construction of hydropower projects in the state. Some of them were in favour of an absolute ban on the cutting of trees, while others were of the opinion that some relaxation may be given for the sake of developmental activities in the region.

Development of the State Due to Hydropower Projects (HPPs)

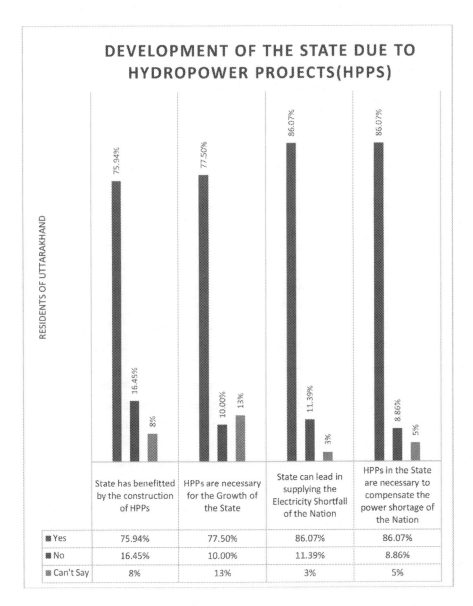

Figure 7

The development of the state due to hydropower projects has been opposed as well as accepted. On being asked if the state had benefitted from the construction of hydropower projects, more than the majority were of the positive view. This is one of the many multiuse benefits of hydropower projects. The synergy between hydropower projects and the growth of the economy has been emphasised. Hydropower projects also have the capacity to provide additional growth benefits. On being asked if hydropower projects are necessary for the growth of the state, a whopping majority—in fact, more than the majority—had a positive reply to the same, making it clear, as a result, that the local populace is a staunch believer in the growth that such projects have to offer. The country as a whole is grappling with the shortfall of power and is finding it difficult to meet current demands. Citizens have to face power cut on a regular basis.

When the respondents were asked if the state can lead in supplying for electricity shortfall of the country, more than majority firmly believed in the same. A large majority of the respondents interviewed were of the opinion that the hydropower projects in the state are necessary to compensate the power shortfall of the nation. Therefore, the hydropower projects in the state can provide an answer for shortfall of power in not just the state but entire country as well.

Hydropower can play a progressive role in facilitating communities to meet power requirements and enable the growth of the state as well as the country. The shortfall of power and its growing needs have been a burning issue and need to be addressed by developing countries like India. Hydropower can provide a green solution to the same. Overall, the question as to whether the development of the state is directly affected by the presence of the hydropower projects in the state, a thumping majority has opined in the positive. It shall be imperative for the state, in the absence of any other major revenue sources, to encourage the development of hydropower. The only caveat is to regulate them so that environmental safeguards may be ensured in pre- and postconstruction activities of the hydropower project.

Large Dams v. Run-of-the-River Projects (RoRs)/
Micro Hydro Projects (MHPs)

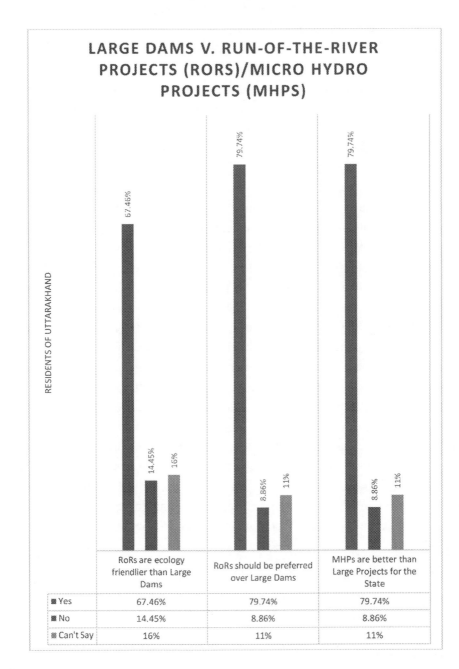

Figure 8

There has been a growing debate between large dams and run-of-the-river projects/micro hydropower projects. Over the years, run-of-the-river hydropower projects have emerged as a more viable and ecologically friendly option to large-scale projects. Majority of the respondents interviewed were of the opinion that run-of-the-river projects are ecologically friendlier than large dams, that they should be preferred over large dams, and that micro hydropower projects are better than large projects for the state. Run-of-the-river hydro projects can create sustainable energy, minimising effects to the environment and communities. Run-of-the-river projects are more feasible as well as environment-friendly, and that is the primary reason that around 80 per cent of residents of Uttarakhand prefer run-of-the-river projects than the large reservoir-based projects. However, during the interviews in some of the Garhwal regions (namely Badasu, Nayalsu, Fata, Khumera, Narayan Koti, Khat, and Khadia of Tehsil Ukhimath in the district of Rudraprayag), the villagers shared a specific problem. Since the last five years and specially during the 16–17 June 2013 calamity, they witnessed a considerable increase in landslides despite there being less than a forty-five-degree slope of land at the western bank of the river Mandakini flowing from Sonprayag to Kund in Tehsil Ukhimath in the district of Rudraprayag. The villagers believe it is because of the tunnels passing beneath the land. It is remarkable that at the western bank, despite being a slope of more than seventy to seventy-five degrees, there are no such landslides in the same region. This needs further investigation by the experts. But prima facie, the tunnels laid by the hydropower company (M/S Lanco Mandakini Hydro Energy Pvt.) may be the reason, as the main allegation of the villagers remained that the proper sealing of the tunnels with the land mass was not done by the company. In the rainy season, that leads to the caving in of the earth's surface.

So if tunnel making is not as per the required scientific standards and due care is not taken by the construction company in the form of proper sealing of tunnels with the adjoining land mass, it may lead o worse results than the large reservoir-based projects. Micro hydro projects are best suitable for local needs.

Rehabilitation by the Hydropower Companies

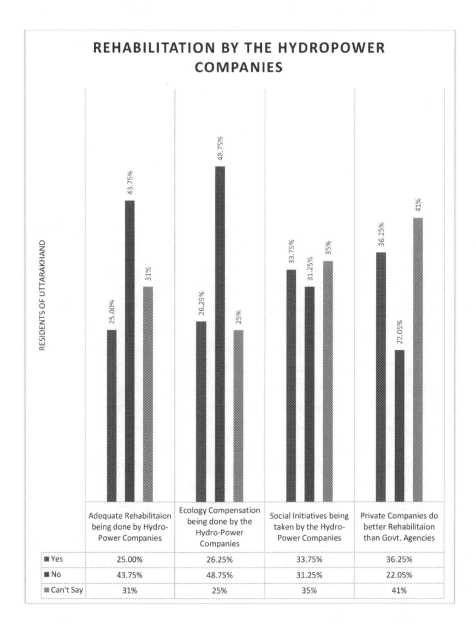

Figure 9

Rehabilitation of people affected by hydropower projects has been an issue of concern. With the growth in energy requirements and the establishment of hydropower projects, many communities face the twin battle of dislocation and rehabilitation.

The rehabilitation packages do not address the complete needs of the community. Accountability mechanisms may be there on paper, where communities can voice their concerns in open meetings, but this is not being implemented in letter and spirit. A negative response was received from 43 per cent of the respondents when asked if adequate rehabilitation was being undertaken by hydropower companies.

The displacement of people due to hydropower projects causes socioeconomic and environmental problems. People may be provided with rehabilitation opportunities, but the environments where they are relocated usually do not align with their skills and resources, causing them further hardship. Around 48 per cent of the respondents were of the opinion that the ecology compensation being done by hydropower companies is not up to mark. Usually, the companies do not adequately compensate for the ecological degradation they have caused. As a result, the ecology suffers, which can have large-scale consequences in future. About 33 per cent of the respondents interviewed believed that the social initiatives taken by the hydropower companies were adequate, whereas 31 per cent replied in the negative. Meanwhile, 41 per cent of the people interviewed did not have an answer when they were asked if private companies do better rehabilitation than government companies, whereas 22 per cent replied in the negative, and 36 per cent replied with a yes.

Rehabilitation cannot be merely in the form of compensation against the land acquired. A peculiar problem in the rehabilitation process was seen during the interview of some of the management officers of the power companies. In the implementation agreement signed with these construction companies, the state government has put all the liability of rehabilitation on the power companies. The dichotomy in law is that for doing rehabilitation and other welfare work, they also need land. Under the present land acquisition scheme, the acquisition of land is primarily done by the state. In the absence of land required, construction companies remain restrained from the required social welfare and rehabilitation responsibilities.

Postconstruction, HPPs Undertake Restoration
of the Loss of the Ecosystem

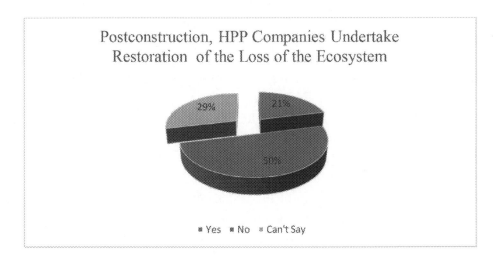

Figure 10

The need for giving back to the environment what hydropower projects have taken should be the main focus of companies involved in hydropower generation. The hydropower industry should invest significant resources in terms of money, time, and manpower to mitigate the negative impacts it has on the environment. There is a need to undertake well-measured and well-planned endeavours to protect and restore the environment, such as the protection of flora and fauna in the region. More often than not, companies do not undertake measures to restore the loss of ecosystems postconstruction of hydropower projects. This has also been stated by 50 per cent of the respondents interviewed. An emergent need appears to preserve ecology by the companies harnessing hydropower and make efforts to restore any damage done in the process. A decisive after-construction environment-friendliness plan needs to be developed by the companies involved in hydropower generation, and environmental auditing should also be considered.

Environment Clearance of Hydropower Projects (HPPs)

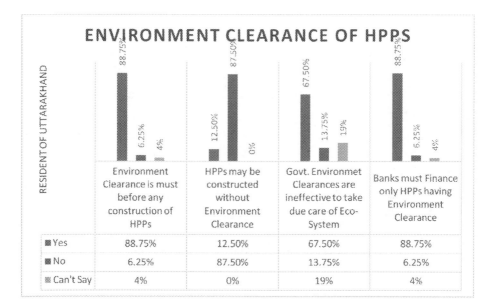

ENVIRONMENT CLEARANCE OF HPPS	Environment Clearance is must before any construction of HPPs	HPPs may be constructed without Environment Clearance	Govt. Environmet Clearances are ineffective to take due care of Eco-System	Banks must Finance only HPPs having Environment Clearance
■ Yes	88.75%	12.50%	67.50%	88.75%
■ No	6.25%	87.50%	13.75%	6.25%
▩ Can't Say	4%	0%	19%	4%

Figure 11

Almost unanimously, people voted that environment clearance for hydropower projects is mandatory. The hon'ble apex court in its order dated 13 August 2013 (*Alaknanda Hydro Power Co. Ltd. v. Anuj Joshi and Others*) held, 'The MoEF as well as State of Uttarakhand not to grant any further environmental clearance or forest clearance for any hydroelectric power project in the State of Uttarakhand, until further orders.' Environmental degradation and hydropower projects have been debated for a long time. The environmental impact of any hydropower project needs to be assessed to make it more viable and sustainable for future use. If environmental concerns outweigh the development benefits, then an incisive view needs to be taken on the issue. About 88 per cent of the respondents were of the view that an environmental clearance is a must before any construction of hydropower projects, whereas 87 per cent were of the view that hydropower projects should not be constructed without an environmental clearance. In response to government-issued environmental clearances being ineffective to take due care of the ecosystem, 67 per cent replied in the affirmative, while 88 per cent believed that the banks should only finance those hydropower projects that have an environmental clearance. Environmental clearances should be decisive and look at the overall impact of the environment.

An environment-impact assessment should be free and fair and done by independent expert bodies. Presently, in almost all hydropower projects, environment-impact assessment reports are commissioned by the hydropower project companies themselves. This leaves a strong bias in favour of the hydropower projects, and often, the environment-impact assessment are not as free and fair as they should be.

It is imperative for the government to do an independent environment-impact assessment of each and every hydropower project. And to further empower expert agencies in the task of monitoring the strict compliance of high environmental standards during the construction and postcommissioning of hydropower projects.

**Opinion regarding Indian Courts' Response
on Hydropower Projects (HPPs)**

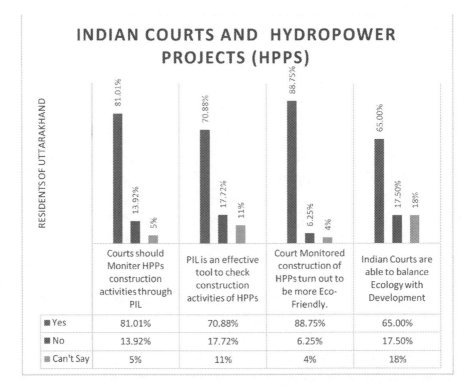

	Courts should Moniter HPPs construction activities through PIL	PIL is an effective tool to check construction activities of HPPs	Court Monitored construction of HPPs turn out to be more Eco-Friendly.	Indian Courts are able to balance Ecology with Development
Yes	81.01%	70,88%	88.75%	65.00%
No	13.92%	17.72%	6.25%	17.50%
Can't Say	5%	11%	4%	18%

Figure 12

Courts have a very important role to play in our society today. Public interest litigations have provided a way for common citizens to approach the courts for the violations of their rights. In keeping with this, courts have intervened. The public has reposed its faith in the judicial system time and again. A total of 81 per cent respondents believed that courts should monitor hydropower project construction activities through public interest litigation, whereas 81 per cent replied in the affirmative that public interest litigation was an effective tool to check construction activities of hydropower projects, and 65 per cent were of the opinion that Indian courts are able to balance ecology and development. The courts have often ordered the formation of expert committees to assess the hydropower projects and their impact on the environment.

The High Court of Uttarakhand at Nainital has played a vital role at all times in the project implementation and monitoring of various hydropower projects in the state. Issues ranging from control on blasting to mining and also the issues of forest clearances have been addressed by the Hon'ble High Court of Uttarakhand through public interest litigation time and again. A major fault all across the implementation process of the hydropower projects of the state is the project monitoring and maintenance of high standards of safety in construction activities. The Hon'ble High Court of Uttarakhand has played a proactive role through public interest petitions in balancing the needs of development with environmental protection in the state. It is remarkable that the high court has checked the haphazard manner of construction whenever possible in the interest of ecological protection, but also for the need of development of the state and its people, it directed the continuance and timely construction of hydropower projects where the state succumbed to the pressures of the seers and sages based on no scientific evidences, merely in the name of pollution of the holy river Ganga. As was the case in *Rural Litigation and Entitlement Kendra (RLEK) v. State of Uttarakhand and Others*,[244] in this case the union government decided to stop construction work on Pala Maneri and Bhairon Ghati, with hydropower projects succumbing under the pressure of the various religious leaders claiming the holiness of the Ganga against that a nongovernment organisation in the state itself filed a public interest petition and prayed for the continuance of run-of-the-river hydropower projects, citing reasons

---

[244] Writ Petition (PIL) 532 of 2008 in the High Court of Uttarakhand at Nainital.

of development of the backward regions of the state. Rural Litigation and Entitlement Kendra (RLEK), based on its own research, brought before the hon'ble high court some glaring facts in its petition that despite having an ambition of an energy-surplus state, there are approximately 1,200 villages in the state that are out of power—a tragic reality of the energy ambition of the state (however, it is pertinent to mention here that the Ministry of Power of the government of India in the 'Quarterly Report of Bharat Nirman: Rural Electrification',[245] as of 31 December 2012, depicts the fact that there is no unelectrified village in the state of Uttarakhand, which is not covered under the Bharat Nirman Rural Electrification Programme). The National Thermal Power Corporation was also successful to an extent in convincing the high court that modern technology and its new method of the run-of-the-river scheme for the construction of hydropower projects are sustainable modes of construction and don't harm the environment and ecology of the area. Considering the facts presented by RLEK and NTPC Ltd., the high court considered the view that not only the concern for the environment and ecology is necessary, but also poverty eradication and development of the backward regions of the state is of importance, so a sustainability approach is to be adopted.[246]

It was remarkable that at the time when almost everybody was succumbing to the pressures of seers and sages based on no scientific evidences, to scrap the hydropower projects in the state and with government offices as high as the prime minister's office and the Ministry of Power were bent on stopping the already half-constructed hydropower projects at Pala Maneri and Bhairon Ghati, the Hon'ble High Court of Uttarakhand took the decision that halting the construction work halfway shall neither be in the interest of the environment nor the development of the state. It was the court's most logical view in the above-mentioned matter that piecemeal approach towards a hydropower project is worse than having them or not having them. A midway halt to construction shall benefit only one party—that is, the contractors involved, whose contract already had a clause that in case of delay or hindrances in government clearance, they shall be compensated, which shall be an utter waste of public money.

---

[245] Data available at the website of the power ministry t: http://powermin.nic.in/bharatnirman/pdf/Unelectrified_Villages.pdf.

[246] Supra note 12.

Opinion on Court Monitoring of Construction Activities of Hydropower Projects (HPPs)

Figure 13

The Indian judiciary has been the torch bearer for the rights of the citizens. As an effective tool for furthering rights, public interest litigation has been a cornerstone of our judiciary. The same view has been confirmed by majority of the respondents of the survey. Almost three-fourth of the respondents have given a positive opinion regarding the court monitoring of the hydropower projects in the state.

Despite of the strong faith reposed by the public in the courts, caveat is that the courts are not the expert bodies for such monitoring. Some innovative systemic change is needed for the effective monitoring of the balance between the right to development and protection of the ecology and environment through courts. Public Interest litigation jurisdiction of the High Courts in the states is required to be strengthened and regulated. Technology transfer is needed to make the courts more efficient and equipped with the mechanism of real time monitoring.

Government v. Private Hydropower Projects (HPPs)

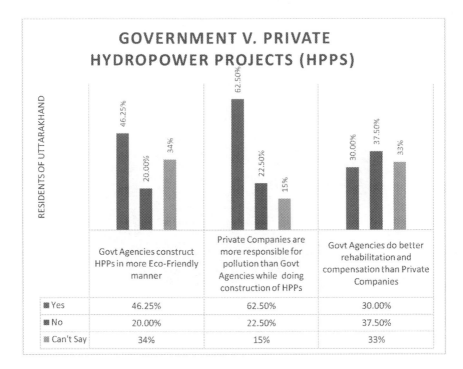

	Govt Agencies construct HPPs in more Eco-Friendly manner	Private Companies are more responsible for pollution than Govt Agencies while doing construction of HPPs	Govt Agencies do better rehabilitation and compensation than Private Companies
■ Yes	46.25%	62.50%	30.00%
■ No	20.00%	22.50%	37.50%
■ Can't Say	34%	15%	33%

Figure 14

There has been no clear understanding of the issue whether government companies provide better opportunities and ecology support than private companies. In Uttarakhand, hydropower projects have been established by both government as well as private sector companies such as National Thermal Power Corporation, GVK, NHPC, etc. When the respondents of Uttarakhand were asked if the government agencies construct hydropower projects in a more eco-friendly manner, 46 per cent replied positively. On being asked if private companies are more responsible for pollution than government agencies while doing construction of hydropower projects, 62 per cent replied in the affirmative. In regard to better rehabilitation and compensation being provided vis-à-vis private and public companies, 30 per cent replied with a yes, 37 per cent with a no, and 33 per cent did not have an answer for the same. The rehabilitation and resettlement offered by companies due to dislocation as a result of hydropower projects need to be based more on needs and should provide the same opportunities and resources that the communities were presented with before. Otherwise, rehabilitating the communities without providing them with economic and social viabilities could pose a threat to their survival.

Man-Made Disaster of 16–17 June 2013
Submerged Srinagar (capital of ancient Garhwal and a big
business town today) in the district of Pauri Garhwal

Picture 1

The June 2013 disaster in the whole of Garhwal, Uttarakhand, shall be long remembered as a tragic memory of the state. It was a classic example when the inefficient and corroded state machinery was caught red-handed unprepared for the wrath of nature. On 16–17 June 2013, in the Garhwal regions of Uttarakhand, heavy rainfall occurred; and for hitherto scientifically unproved reasons, heavy flooding occurred in almost all the river systems of the region, starting from the Kedarnath Temple until the lower regions as far as Haridwar. As a routine failure, and shamefully so, the state government to date has not been able to successfully carry out any detailed scientific study on the reasons for the said disaster. Thousands of people died not because of the disaster but because the state was unprepared for such a disaster. People died on the road with cold. People died due to the lack of medical aid. People hoping for rescue died in despair. One thing is certain out of all this uncertainty: that it was not a natural disaster—it was surely a man-made one. We created this disaster and waited for nature to trigger it. That is what happened in the Kedarnath valley on 16–17 June 2014. As per the guesswork of many government agencies, the tragedy happened mainly because of the bursting of Chorabari Lake above the Kedarnath valley. Only ordinary prudence is needed to understand that an isolated incident of a lake burst cannot fill more than twenty feet of water in all the river valleys of the whole Garhwal region.

**Riverside home washed away, Agastyamuni
in the district of Rudaprayag**

Picture 2

Development in the hill regions must be done with a caveat in mind for the respect of nature. Obstructing the course of nature shall evidently result into such disasters. A scientific analysis of the causes of the 16–17 June 2013 excessive flooding of the rivers may require a much bigger and wider study than this one. Violation of environmental laws by hydropower project construction companies as well as the local people mainly living in the riverbanks is rampant in the state, which has resulted in this disaster.

Pandukeshwar Temple half hanging in the river, Vishnuprayag in the district of Chamoli

Picture 3

The temple in the picture was in fact constructed by the J. P. Hydro Power Construction Company during their Vishnuprayag hydropower project in the district of Chamoli. Today, all but this remnant has gone down the river. If only there was no violation of the existing guidelines on the riverbanks, many lives could have been saved.

Major roads of the whole Garhwal region washed away

Picture 4

Devastated Agastyamuni in the district of Rudraprayag

Picture 5

In the absence of any scientific study to the contrary, it shall not be wise to reach to the conclusion that hydropower projects in the valley are the soul curse behind the disaster of 16–17 June 2013 in the state. But it is a fact that haphazard construction activity of any kind—be it hydropower projects in the valley, heavy silting of construction material on riverbanks, unscientific blasting activity by the construction companies, and also the heavy encroachments of human settlements on the riverbanks—is the primary reason behind such disasters.

Lessons to Be Learnt

1.   Independent environment-impact assessment and monitoring

Almost all environment-impact assessments done for various hydropower projects in the state were commissioned by the same hydropower projects for which they were doing the assessment. An element of bias can never be ruled out from such a system of assessment. It may be difficult to give findings against their own financer even if the assessment agency finds some faults. It is imperative for the government to have environment-impact assessment done for each and every project in the state from an independent agency with no financial or administrative dependence on the hydropower project company from which it is doing the assessment. Presently, monitoring part of the construction and allied activities undertaken by the hydropower project companies is completely missing in the state. There is no monitoring mechanism to ensure that hydropower companies undertake the construction activities within the contractual framework. Many public interest petitions have been filed in the Hon'ble High Court of Uttarakhand just to ensure that the construction companies do not undertake blasting activities outside permissible limits. Issues related to air, water, and noise pollution remain unchecked during the construction work; and people are left at the mercy of the district administration, which apparently is unequipped with the technical issues involved and devoid of any such monitoring powers over the hydropower projects in the area. Even after the commissioning, constant monitoring is required for the hydropower projects in the state. Improper muck disposal by the hydropower construction companies was one of the major reasons for the change in the river course during the June,2013 natural calamity in the state. A proper monitoring mechanism may ensure such matters like muck disposal and minimum environmental flow are maintained by the hydropower projects. At present, in the state, there is no monitoring system in place for assessing the impact of hydropower projects on the wildlife and aquatic life of the river; it can only be done by a constant monitoring system in place.

Therefore,

A. a new environment-impact assessment and monitoring authority may be constituted.
B. to make a new environment-impact assessment authority autonomous as act, it should be passed by the legislative assembly of the state of Uttarakhand.

2.   Cascading effect assessment (CEA)

In addition to a separate environmental impact assessment for each and every hydroelectricity project, a cascading effect assessment must also be done if more than one hydroelectricity project is being sanctioned on the same river basin. The carrying capacity of the river must be assessed before sanctioning a new project on the same river. Another bad effect of the cascading hydropower project on the same river at very short distance is that it results into the fragmentation of the river flow and hampers the capacity of the river water to return the modified natural factors to normal levels before it reaches the next reservoir. Each cascading impediment with no sufficient time gap for the water to return to normal chemistry ultimately kills the whole biodiversity of the river water by the time it reaches the ultimate downstream. So a cascading effect assessment (CEA) is very necessary for the whole river basin having multiple projects in addition to the separate environment-impact assessment of each and every hydropower project.

Therefore,

A. a cascading effect assessment must be done before sanctioning hydropower project on the same river at very short distance.

B. the carrying capacity of the river must be assessed and taken care of before sanctioning more than one hydro project on the same river stream.

3. Sustainability bonus and green tax

Export of energy from the state must entail special green tax on the importers. Most of the large hydropower projects in the state were contemplated with the view to produce and export with a very minor share to local residents of the state. Natural disasters like that of June 2013 and serious financial crunch faced by the state government for reconstruction and rehabilitation have changed the idea considerably. At the time of such crises, it is the local populace of the state who will bear the fury of nature. Whether various hydropower projects were the direct cause of such a disaster is yet to be scientifically established, but the fact that cannot be denied is that the presence of a large number of hydropower projects and haphazard construction activities induced by them were certainly the aggravating factor in the natural disaster of June 2013. In such a scenario, the local populace of the state has an entrenched right of first use in any kind of hydroelectricity production. For each and every export of electricity, a sustainability bonus must be given to the local community. The state must keep a sustainability bonus clause in all its memoranda of understanding in favour of the local community and should impose green tax on hydropower production in the state. In Uttarakhand, the lack of medical facilities is a major problem in the remote areas. As a sustainability bonus, it may be made imperative for hydropower companies to maintain high-standard health facilities in the form of hospitals for the local population, and a green tax may be levied to fund schools in remote river valleys.

Therefore,

A. new legislation from the state legislature should be enacted defining the sustainability bonus and procedure for quantifying it for the local populace.
B. the state must keep a sustainability bonus clause in all its memoranda of understanding with the hydropower construction companies and pay quantifiable monetary benefits to the local community.

C. in order to make rehabilitation smoother, a rehabilitation clause in the implementation agreement with the hydropower companies must contain land acquisition details to be done by state agencies for the purpose of rehabilitation work.

D. private as well as government companies should be audited for testing their construction and allied activities on sustainable development principles.

4.   Only companies with core competence in hydropower should be commissioned.

Hydropower project construction companies having very little or no experience in the area of hydropower projects are one of the major causes of concern. In the state of Uttarakhand, a large number of mushrooming the hydropower projects have been because of various new and inexperienced hydropower companies with no scale of operation and modern technology transfer to their credit. Projects have also been sanctioned for the companies who have no successful track record in the field of hydropower generation. The figure below shows the benefits of construction companies having core competence in hydropower:

Benefits of Core-Competence Construction Companies

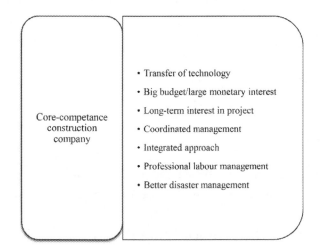

Figure 1

It cannot be a mere coincidence that a state like Uttarakhand boasting such vast hydropower potential failed to attract world leaders in energy-production business and that majority of small-, medium-, or large-scale hydropower projects are being implement by indigenous companies with little technology transfer to their credit. They employ new and inexperienced techniques of construction that fail to pass the test of nature at a time like 16–17 June 2013, when a number of small hydropower projects could not withstand the flow of the river and were completely washed away.

During a field visit to the construction site of a hydropower project being built by the GVK Company at Shrinagar (in the district of Pauri), it was observed that a huge number of migrant labourers were employed by the construction company without even providing them basic facilities like housing and sanitation. Consequently, every morning, there was a long queue of people squatting for toilet at the riverbank. There was no cleaning mechanism employed by the above-mentioned construction company. All the sewage directly went into river (which has a huge religious value for the people) without any treatment. Thus, migration of labour must be taken care of, and construction companies must also be scrutinised based on the best labour practices. The figure below brings out the core competence that construction companies should refer to.

Therefore,

A. companies having core competence in hydropower project construction should be given preference while selecting companies for implementing projects.
B. an implementation agreement should contain a 'transfer of technology' clause to ensure the use of the latest and most efficient technologies of construction as well as disaster management.
C. companies having a large scale of economies should be given preference to ensure the most long-term interest in the project.
D. squatting and toilets at riverbanks by migrant labourers should be checked, and each municipality should make by-laws for sanitation activities of a large migrant labour population.

5.　　**Government power companies should be given preference over private construction companies.**

One major reason cited against government companies is the huge delay in the construction and commissioning of hydropower projects (e.g. the Tehri Hydro Power Project). It took more than thrice the estimated time and cost in construction and then final commissioning of the project. But the solidity of construction and the ingenuity of the design, which withstood the scale of disaster like that of 16–17 June 2013 (in Garhwal, Uttarakhand), surely justify the inordinate delay and cost of the construction. The figure below connotes such benefits:

Benefits of Government Construction Companies

Government Construction Companies

- Most long-term interest in projects
- Better checks and balances in system
- Subtle profit motives
- Better labour practices
- Better likelihood to adherence to sustainable standards
- Directly answerable to the government
- Better likelihood of coordination with state machinery

Figure 2

It may not be out of place to mention that the Tehri Dam was ever designed for the flood-moderation function; still, it considerably checked the disastrous flow of the river during the disaster like that of 16–17 June 2013. At the same time, many newly constructed and under-construction small hydropower projects could not face the same test of nature. Contrary to popular belief, government companies are able to perform and deliver much better than their private counterparts in the long term.

Therefore,

A. to ensure most long-term interests in the projects and to ensure subtle profit motives, government hydropower companies must be preferred over private construction companies.

B. state legislature should enact for the constitution of new hydropower companies having specific sections mandating sustainable development principles.

C. existing enactments like that for Tehri Hydro Development Corporation should be amended, commitment to sustainable development principles should be added in its preamble, and specific sections should be added, making adherence to sustainable development principles as a statutory duty of government companies.

6. Integrated approach for hydropower projects

In the state of Uttarakhand, the hydropower sector is a highly fragmented sector. An integrated approach to the construction of hydropower projects in the state should be developed. Instead of various small- and medium-scale construction companies, large and reputed hydropower projects construction companies who can develop a holistic plan to the hydropower potential of the river should be involved. Various small projects having no integrated approach are susceptible to causing more environmental harm than developmental good to the area. Companies having core competence in hydropower generation surely bring a large scale of operation and naturally have a long-term interest in the projects. It brings better construction techniques with the latest technology transfer and coordinated management. Fragmentation of the whole sector has led to chaos and faulty implementation of the projects. A small scale of operation of many small- and medium-sized companies does not often allow them to meet the highest standards of the industry. The absence of international companies having worldwide experience of the construction of hydropower projects is a matter more of suspense than worry. It may also be in the interest of the state and sustainable power generation to gain from the expertise and experience of the big international firms to facilitate 'transfer of technology' in this area.

Therefore,

A. in order to check fragmentation of the whole sector that has led to chaos and faulty implementation of projects instead of various small- and medium-scale construction companies, large and reputed hydropower projects construction companies should be commissioned.

7.   Hydropower projects through a cooperative model

The direct stakes of the people should be increased in construction companies. A cooperative company model should be promoted. Instead of one-time compensation, local people may be given an option of deferred compensation/share in the construction company or an interest in any future revenue generation. It may have twin benefits. One shall be that compensation burden will be less for the hydropower company. Second, when local people have direct involvement/stakes in the project, they will be more participatory in nature. Such a model of construction project shall be mutually beneficial for the local people as well as for the hydropower companies. The model of a construction project is provided below in figure 4.

Therefore,

A. to ensure the increased participation of the local people, construction companies should be asked to adopt cooperative structure.
B. to connect local people with the future of the hydropower project, shareholding of *gram sabha*/local body in the proposed revenue generation should be ensured.

8.   Separate grievance redressal system

At present, the district administration or, in exceptional matters, high courts through public interest petitions are generally the only authorities to address all or any grievances with regard to hydropower projects. Certainly, there is no formal system in place for disposing complaints and redressing grievances of the nature warranting specific scientific investigations neither there are any disaster specific laws and adjudicatory institutions in the state which can deal with such matters, like the caving in of the land, reservoir-induced slope instabilities, damages from blasting, cattle loss, or any other kind of loss due to the construction and operation of hydroelectricity projects in the area. District administration officials often may not be subject experts and sometime may also carry an element of bias in favour of the hydropower companies due to their economic and social influence in the area. It is advisable to have a separate grievance redressal system in place, having expert members equipped with investigating powers and separate laws to deal with such kinds of complaints. Public interest petitions cannot be a substitute for an executive/quasi-judicial grievance redressal system for these matters. Neither the courts are subject experts on hydropower and incidental issues, nor their procedures are elaborate enough to warrant scientific investigation in each and every complaint of such nature.

Therefore,

A. state legislature should enact law making construction-related accidents penal in nature, like that of the caving in of land, reservoir-induced slope instabilities, damages from blasting, cattle loss, or any other kind of loss due to the construction and operation of hydroelectricity projects in the area.
B. the state government should ensure a separate grievance redressal system in place, having expert members equipped with investigating powers and separate laws to deal with complaints related to construction activities as mentioned above.
C. an independent regulatory commission should be established to ensure sustainable development standards in the postconstruction functioning of hydropower companies (for example, ensuring the minimum flow of river).

9. Strict scrutiny of 'public interest' by the courts

Public interest petitions must be strictly scrutinised by the courts. Interestingly, the study of the court cases against hydropower companies in the High Court of Uttarakhand filed in the form of public interest litigation revealed that most of public interest petitions were filed against government companies. On an interview with the people in the areas in which private construction companies are operating, it came out that private construction companies pay money for whatever damage is claimed by the villagers (and add it to their construction cost), which prevents villagers from approaching the high court for raising any public interest pretence. On the contrary, public sector companies have no such free hand in compensation distribution; and before any compensation is given, damage has to be ascertained (often not as high as given by private companies), and that leads to more and more public interest petitions against public sector companies by disgruntled villagers. The fact remains that fewer people actually come to the court for public interest; rather, it is the unfulfilled private interest that is often scored under the garb of a public interest petition against the power company. One law officer of NTPC Ltd. interviewed for this research candidly confessed to the fact that in Uttarakhand, their engineers are busier in fighting court cases than in engineering work. Certainly, this is not the best scenario to work for a hydropower construction company. Public interest jurisdiction of the constitutional courts in the country (by *suo motu* relaxing the principle of *locus standi*) till the time it is linked with article 32 and article 226 of the Constitution of India cannot be interfered with by the executive or the legislature in any manner. It is the need of the hour that such 'all encompassing' jurisdiction should be regulated by way of clear guidelines and statutory regulations inserting procedural safeguards for all parties.

Therefore,

A. Pleadings with regard to the bonafide of the petitioner in the public interest petition may be made mandatory in the first paras of the petition to ensure genuine public interest petitions.

B. Declaration on oath before the court be made mandatory for all the petitioners in the public interest petitions stating that the public interest petition is not being filed to target any specific private party.

10. Panchayats (Extension to the Scheduled Areas) (PESA) Act of 1996 to enhance direct decision making

Most remote areas where hydropower projects are being set up in the state or are proposed often do not have a very large local population. Due to the small local population, there is a possibility of involving people in the decision-making process. Local people are the worst affected in case any tragedy like that of 16–17 June 2013 happens, so they have the highest stake in the construction of hydropower projects in their area. In addition to the cooperative model of a construction company, local people can also be involved in the decision making with regard to land acquisition, compensation, etc. People must be informed about the pros and cons of such hydropower projects first, and then their opinion must be taken into account before making decisions for or against the development of the area. Panchayats (Extension to the Scheduled Areas) Act of 1996 was enacted to enable tribal self-rule. The act extended the provisions of panchayats (seventy-third constitutional amendment) to tribal areas that fall under the Fifth Schedule areas. The act does not extend to the state of Uttarakhand. The act provides that 'the Gram Sabha or the Panchayats at the appropriate level shall be consulted before making the acquisition of land in the Scheduled Areas for development projects and before re-settling or rehabilitating persons affected by such projects in the Scheduled Areas' (section 4 [i]). A similar step can be taken up by amending the State Panchayati Raj Act. This will enable the *gram sabha* to have a decisive voice in the setting up of hydropower projects and the subsequent rehabilitation of affected communities. The *gram sabha*, which is seen as the cornerstone of local governance, will provide a voice to local communities in the setting up of such hydropower projects. Further, this will also act as an accountability mechanism whereby local people can voice their concerns. A kind of direct democracy, which will enhance participation of local people in the decision making process; and instead of project sanctioning by shareholders like officials and capital investors, it will provide say in the sanctioning of the hydro projects directly from the stakeholders, i.e., the 'local community'.

Therefore,

A. the Panchayats (Extension to the Scheduled Areas) Act of 1996 should be extended and implemented in the state of Uttarakhand.
B. implementation agreements with the hydropower companies of the state of Uttarakhand should contain land acquisition details and responsibilities for rehabilitation purposes.